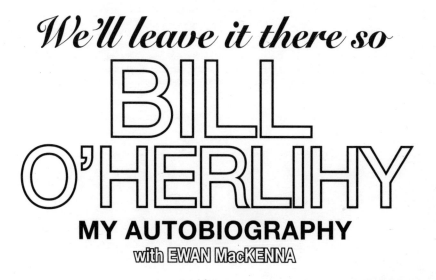

We'll leave it there so

BILL O'HERLIHY

MY AUTOBIOGRAPHY
with EWAN MacKENNA

Paperweight

First published in 2012 by Paperweight Publications, Level 4, Building 5,
Dundrum Townhouse Centre, Dublin 16, Ireland.

9781908813060
'We'll Leave It There So' - The Bill O'Herlihy Autobiography

9781908813114
'We'll Leave It There So' - The Bill O'Herlihy Autobiography e-book

Printed and bound by CPI Group
(UK) Ltd, Croydon, CR0 4YY

Paperweight Publishing Group, Level 4, Building 5,
Dundrum Townhouse Centre, Dublin 16, Ireland.

www.paperweightpublications.ie

Dedication

To the three women in my life
– Hilary, Jill and Sally –
Loving, Loyal, Inspiring

Bill O'Herlihy, 2012

CONTENTS

FOREWORD

By EAMON DUNPHY

BILL O'Herlihy has been part of my life for a long time.

We first worked together on RTÉ's coverage of the 1978 World Cup, but I'd heard plenty about Bill before then.

He was one of the best known journalists in Ireland from his time on the '7 Days' programme.

RTE's soccer coverage over nearly four decades wouldn't have been the same — or as effective — without Bill. It helped greatly that he had a background in current affairs, rather than in sports journalism.

The world of Irish sports journalism at the time was cosy, clubbable and full of fans with typewriters.

But the forensic approach that RTÉ allowed us to take to soccer coverage played a part in changing the culture.

Getting John Giles on board for the 1986 World Cup was a huge plus, but so too was Bill's role.

For a panel to click and bounce off each other and to make for good television, then the host is vitally important.

He has to know what questions to ask, when to ask them, when a follow-up question is needed.

And, crucially, he needs to learn when to shut up and just let the discussion flow.

Bill has few peers anywhere in anchoring sports discussions — on RTÉ's Olympic Games programmes as well as the soccer coverage.

It's never about controversy for controversy's sake. It's

about driving debate, confronting issues and digging deeper.

There have been times when myself or Liam Brady, in particular, have got a bit annoyed with some of Bill's questions. But then you see that cute Cork glint in his eye and you realise that he's got what he wanted.

Bill has lived life to the full. Raising a wonderful family and growing a highly successful public relations company.

Like all Leesiders, he's never forgotten where he came from, and insists on reminding us regularly of the superiority of Corkonians. We've argued plenty over the years. About politics, sport, everything really.

We mightn't always agree, but Bill is someone I respect greatly.

He is a brilliant broadcast journalist and asks the questions that people want answered.

There are so many spoofers on air and in print these days, but Bill cuts to the chase.

He does his homework, and prepares as diligently now as he did 34 years ago.

It's a peculiar quirk that many people disagreed with what I said about Jack Charlton during Italia '90 but they kept tuning in.

John Giles made similar criticisms of Jack but was a bit more temperate in the way he phrased things.

It seemed that Irish people actually took pride in the fact that we were willing to rock the boat.

There was none of the cosy familiarity and fear of offending someone that you get on other channels.

Bill played a crucial role in growing the popularity of RTÉ's soccer coverage. Some other presenters might have run scared of any criticism of Jack etc, but Bill knew there were issues that needed to be discussed.

He's been threatening to retire for a while now, but the finishing line must be in sight somewhere over the horizon if he's publishing an autobiography.

Or maybe he's just annoyed that John got in ahead of him!

I've worked with Bill for close on 35 years, and there hasn't been a day that I've dreaded heading into the studio.

He indulges us at times, but Bill's professionalism never dims.

Bill does more preparation than anyone. He has the same work ethic now as he did when he started out in journalism with the 'Cork Examiner'.

Leave it there so? ... I'll believe it when I see it.

CHAPTER 1

Lights, Camera, Action...

In Three. Two. One.

I love live television. The quiet seconds where you can hear your heartbeat outrun the countdown to air, finally reaching a crescendo as the pent-up nerves suddenly burst free and you go out in real time to hundreds of thousands of viewers. It's inspiring and I much prefer it to anything pre-recorded. I'd like to think my performance is about 10 times better as well, because live television is about an adrenaline surge and not worrying about making mistakes. Some people tense up at the thought of a blunder and maybe they are not made for this because therein lies the key. Should mistakes occur, you just remind yourself that this is live, not always squeaky-clean, sanitised and unnatural. You can say something that's wrong or mispronounced and it's not ideal but so what? Be yourself and forget about it.

Often, I'm not the best when it comes to names, and I think I've a bit of a reputation for that but I just go with it. I remember covering an Olympic Games way back in 1980 in Moscow and I said, "Well thank God for this, here comes a name I can really pronounce. The gold medal in fencing has gone to Smirnoff". I was delighted with this, thinking of the vodka as I reeled off the syllables, although closer inspection of the Russian athlete afterwards made me realise I was in fact wrong again. It was Smirnov. Indeed, just a few minutes ago, I was looking through the teamsheet for tonight's game and I quickly noted that there are a few player names I'll be hoping to avoid. But mess up and it confirms to people it's live and that you can sink or swim.

A couple of weeks back I was settling comfortably into our Wednesday night Champions League coverage when suddenly my phone went off in my pocket. It was my wife Hilary who presumed it would be turned off but wanted to leave a message. I think she got as much of a shock as I did when she got through. It was an elementary mistake on my part and it was made clear I was long enough in the game to know better. Anyone watching could have heard the ringtone but people take comfort from imperfection. And all the variables that go with live television get the adrenaline racing. There's nothing quite like it, and even all these years into my broadcasting career, the thrill remains every bit as sharp and cutting and raw.

Way back when I was starting out in this game, before he became a Labour TD, even a nationally-renowned broadcaster like David Thornley sometimes struggled to contain that onrush of excitement and he was known to have a glass of brandy before he went on air. When I mentioned that story to Liam Brady, he told me that during his playing days with Arsenal, for home games, there was always a bottle of brandy in their dressing room too. It was up to individual players as to whether they took a drink or not, not that anyone would have been lashing into it. But it was part and parcel of the game-day equipment and seen as a benefit to those with a certain, perhaps more fragile, mentality. Be it Highbury or RTÉ, it was all about soothing nerves.

That's long gone though. Nothing but water and soft drinks are available and they have all been whisked away moments before we go on air. Eamon Dunphy had a stack of cans of Coke beside him as he chewed on a home-made curry, having admonished everyone else at the pre-show meeting for eating the cafeteria food that, he suggested, good humouredly, "was at a cost to the taxpayer so all of you should be ashamed of yourselves". John Giles and Brady got through a few gallons of tea, the lads knowing well not to take the bait and let their colleague get under their skin so early into the evening. Meanwhile behind the desk everyone can see at home, a small table sits beside me, out of view of the camera, dotted like a chess board with empty cups of tea. It's almost a routine at this stage, granted not a particularly healthy one, and the glasses of water in front of us all are little more than decorative and remain largely untouched.

"Good evening," I say as the countdown ends and I stare into the camera lens. "It's been quite a season so far." And with that, we are up and running. In my earpiece I can hear the editor in the gallery as he sends down instructions and suggestions from on high. English by birth, Eugene O'Neill is laid back and quiet around the office but he's highly competent, imaginative and somehow takes all the various and vastly differing strands of this show and makes them fit seamlessly together. A pleasure to work with. In my left ear, I try to keep track of his production instructions, while out of my right ear I must keep on top of the panel's conversation so I can prod and jab at their words like a piñata, in the hope of getting the best out of them and quite possibly a reaction as well.

As the programme swings into action, Dunphy takes tonight's home team and swiftly guides the audience through their strengths and weaknesses. Brady takes the visitors and does likewise. Giles talks over a couple of clips he picked out earlier in the day, long before any of us arrived in Montrose because that's his way. On match-days, he's often out here in RTÉ in the early morning and he is meticulous, pays huge attention to detail and his highlights demonstrate exactly what he wants to get across. He is the ultimate professional, the best analyst on any channel, and hasn't become lazy in all the time he's been doing this.

He talks about tactics and the influence they'll have on the upcoming game but I'm also aware that our pre-match time is short tonight and Eugene reminds me with a sense of urgency that we are tight up against a break. It's fine though because it's Giles in full flow and he knows my signals when I want him to stop. Giles, Dunphy and myself have worked together for so many years that they know when I signal they must stop before I cut across them. Brady, though, has a different style and it's not as easy to cut across him. I realised that when he first came in here to us for the 1998 World Cup. Once he starts making his point, he always has to finish. If I cut across his comment, he is likely to talk over me in a slightly louder tone. I can understand that completely in a football sense but television discipline has its own demands and I've just got to live with it – most especially since his comment is always good.

"Alright," I say, "we have to take a commercial break there but we'll be back with all the first half action after that." And from there it's time to co-ordinate with upstairs. "We'll be taking the third insert presumably after the break?" I ask Eugene in the gallery as he and the others working out of sight quickly calculate time. The lads beside me patiently await the answer because of the possibility of more face time, as they like to call it. Dunphy feels he has drawn the short straw in the opening segment and was feeding on crumbs. He wants to use the third insert, primarily to be fair, because he believes it's relevant to the game.

I'm comfortable with Dunphy no matter how much he may press for face time. Eamon is good humoured, professional, disciplined in production terms. I've learned how to deal with him over the course of 34 years sitting in various studios in this place, nattering back and forth about every topic imaginable while a game played out on a television screen in front of us. But I have huge admiration too, not just because he has taken punditry to a new cerebral level that's completely above the normal level of soccer comment, but because of where he had to come from.

Way back in the mid-1970s, the doors of this place and indeed all journalism institutions were closed to Dunphy. He had just left Shamrock Rovers after a year and had no stamps, no savings and was stony broke as he put it himself. Plus, wanting to get into journalism seemed a waste of time because you couldn't get an NUJ card unless you had work published and you couldn't get work published unless you had an NUJ card. It was catch-22 but rather than taking a gently, gently approach, he kicked those closed doors right down as only he could and he really announced his arrival through the television medium come the World Cup in Argentina in 1978.

At the time the brilliant Tim O'Connor had a major role in television sport and he, with Mike Horgan, transformed the soccer landscape. Both were hugely important in my development as a broadcaster in sport, both had confidence in me when many others did not and both nurtured my career in a way which is impossible to repay. Tim subsequently became Head of Sport and he was the man who negotiated rights for World Cups and European soccer as he strove to develop RTÉ's pretty limited sports coverage of the time. But if he helped me and RTÉ, he helped Dunphy in a huge way too.

Tim had himself been a very good print journalist and had started in the Independent, and by then the Sunday World sports section was sub-contracted out to him as a package. He gave Dunphy a column in that package and he must have been impressed with what he read because soon after he asked him if he'd like to go onto television. So Dunphy and I began to work together, just the two of us in a small studio but with a huge amount of time to fill because we had either limited or no commercial breaks. I thought he was terrific but I saw quickly the underlying steel.

It wasn't enough for Dunphy to merely be on television. Sometimes I reminisce with him about this and he's typically cutting about what RTÉ were doing back then. At that stage, for World Cups, the coverage here in studio consisted of a massive set, with Liam Nolan in a white suit at one end of it, and me at the other end. In between the two of us, as if to contrast with the present, Dunphy still says "there were a couple of hacks who didn't know what they were talking about". He didn't want to be a part of that, and even though he really needed the work, as he saw it, it had to be on his terms and it had to be done right.

He wasn't prepared to participate in what he saw as mediocrity so he came to me first and later to Tim with a radical idea that might have seemed to some to be above his station. He told both of us that we should have analysis rather than comment and he wanted to take clips of a game like we do now, use his expertise to go over them and let me use my journalistic ability to find the story. He was straight out with it too. "Let's do it this way," I remember him telling Tim all those years ago. "Get rid of these buffoons who don't know what they are talking about. They are a waste of space. And you don't need that big set either. That should go as well."

Tim went for it. It was a hard sell but Tim was a smart guy and he liked that Dunphy was happy to put himself right out there where people could easily come back at him and have a serious cut. That had never been done before and it ended up with just Dunphy and I doing those 1978 World Cup broadcasts from the small presentation studio where the entire operation was scaled right down and it was so much better for it. That was the beginnings of where we are tonight.

He won the battle then, but now, his demands won't be met as word comes from the gallery about the timing of the next segment. It's going to be a quick handover to the commentary team of George Hamilton and Ray Houghton. "Yeah, George really needs more time to talk alright, he's only going to be doing it for over an hour and a half," says Dunphy. But he knows it won't change a thing and he grumbles briefly while more instructions pour down like a waterfall and into my earpiece.

I'm one of the few presenters who likes open talkback during a live show. It's based on the belief that if there's a problem looming I want to know about it immediately. I got caught once without it and it taught me a lesson. I was anchoring 'Sports Stadium' with a keyed or mainly closed talkback when director Joe McCormack blasted into my ear "we've got a problem, lead me to a commercial break". Which I did. We were due to go to Kirkistown in Northern Ireland for live motor racing but a sudden rainstorm disrupted their programme and the race was put back for 30 minutes.

Thirty-minute delay equals a 30-minute gap in a live programme. And we had so little time as the commercial break was a mere 34 seconds. "What have we got to fill Joe, and what are we going to do?" I asked. "I'll tell you what you're going to do, son. You're going to do what you're paid to do.

Talk. And you're going to keep talking and if you have a problem I'll send in a straw hat and a cane and give you the key of C." Some comedian Joe.

Back on the air, I talked for 10 minutes about soccer before they found a filler until the race began. I got a round of applause from the studio crew but I vowed never again would I be caught like that. If I had realised there was a problem looming I would have been better prepared. From then on an open talkback for me.

It means, of course, you are exposed to multiple conversations in your ear – between the director, the insert editors, those manning an OB, graphics, the editor and his people and your own instructions when appropriate but after that day, it was a small price to pay.

****

I found it difficult to listen to multiple conversations at the start, especially when there was so much talking in my ear as I conducted interviews in the studio. Hilary often asks me how I do it and I just tell her that you get more and more used to it over time. In fact I'm so used to it these days that all the interference and noise bouncing around me calms me a little now and gives me a split second to flit back in time. It's then I realise that if the formation of this panel and this show has been down to luck in many ways, so has my own evolution.

So, sitting here and feeling nostalgic tonight, I see a nervous and skinny, dark-haired boy not long past his 16th birthday in the offices of the Cork Examiner. He's keeping his head down and trying to get by. It's 1954 and he's desperate to be a journalist but sometimes looks out of place because of his age and I think about my journey from there to here, then to now, him to me. I consider too the series of chance events over my lifetime that have left me feeling so fortunate about everything I have done and where I have ended up, because that nervous and skinny, dark-haired boy has lived out and continues to live out his dream. If I could talk to him, I don't think I could give him any advice or tell him to do anything differently because it all worked out for him. For the most part anyway. The road was winding and most of the time he didn't know what was around the bend but he got on with it and despite a few scares, ended up where he wanted to be - which, right now, is calling the shots in Studio Four of RTÉ.

Sometimes it's important to contemplate the journey on which one has travelled. And most lunchtimes on a break from my public relations business, I find myself at Mass in the nearby St Mary's Church, Haddington Road. And then, just as now, I think of the very starting point and where I grew up on the Glasheen Road. When I was a kid it was on the western edge of Cork, although now it's nestled in amongst the suburbs, and it was there I was born into a family full of love. I was blessed and maybe that's the primary reason that has allowed me to make it all this way because in many ways it's one's childhood and upbringing that shapes and hones a person.

I recall where that love came from and remember my father who was an extremely hard-working public servant. Initially a clerical officer in St Finbarr's Hospital, he went on to take charge of the administrative side of the Orthopedic Hospital. The only part of life he took more seriously than his work was perhaps his religion and not just in the sense of going to Mass, but putting what he believed into practice. He was a member of the Lough Parish Sick-Poor Society and he'd collect every Sunday and I often did that with him. That was our time together and he had a huge area around a big development called Greenmount and rain or shine he would go every week, door to door, collecting coins for the poor.

He did it for years and years and the Lough Parish was the first to introduce meals on wheels in Cork even though they never got credit - that went to a more high-profile city group who were good people who also knew how to cultivate publicity. Not that publicity was the reason he started it and not that it ever bothered him in the slightest.

Dad was an extraordinarily generous person in terms of his relationships with those around him and he was one of these rarities in that he always saw the good in others. Of course there was the occasional exception and my brother Jack sometimes reminds me that there was a picture of the Sacred Heart positioned in our dining room and it had what we kids called 'moving eyes'. If we ever did something wrong and our parents wanted to get at the truth, you had to stand in front of that picture and be honest. And you told the truth then because you had those eyes staring through you no matter which way you sidestepped and it was quite intimidating. That will give you a sense of how discipline was partly based on religion in our house.

When we were young, we could not eat the night before we went to Communion either. In other words, Saturday midnight was the last time you could eat until after Sunday Mass. But one time, the folks were entertaining some people which would have been a rare occasion, let me tell you, and Jack came down early morning and ate some leftovers. There was suspicion, correctly aimed at him, and he was made stand in front of the Sacred Heart picture and told to apologise. Straight out, he refused to do it. My father then said, "Okay, if that's the way you feel about it, I'll march you up to Greenmount".

Greenmount was an industrial school on the southside of Cork city and had an horrendous reputation. Being landed in that place was the biggest threat that could be made against us. Of course we didn't know you couldn't just walk up and be handed in, you had to be sent by the Courts. So my father went upstairs, packed Jack's suitcase and marched him up towards the door and Jack would not back down. It ended with him being told just to not do it again and my father actually lost out but it's the furthest the Greenmount threat ever went.

But religious discipline wasn't an all-consuming part of our young lives and it's so innocent now looking back. I wouldn't want under any circumstances to convey the impression that my father and mother were raving, fascist Catholics, they certainly were not. If you know you are loved, which we did, and you made a mistake and were punished for it, that was fine by us. It was part of the balance of life and we all grew to understand that.

My father loved sport too. He was a good oarsman and won rowing trophies with the Cork Boat Club but football and particularly hurling were his passions. In fact as the lads in the studio beside me talk about the match ahead, I remember that soccer wasn't even my first sport because I have a torrent of memories that involve going down to the Athletic Grounds, the Park as we knew it then, now Páirc Uí Chaoimh. It was a golden era for Cork hurling. We had Christy Ring, who I saw many times for Cork and Glen Rovers, Seán Condon, who was a great player for my parish team, the Barrs, and captained the county to minor and senior All-Irelands, Tom Mulcahy, who was a fabulous All Ireland-winning goalie, and the iconic Paddy Barry of Sarsfields. As well as visiting greats like Mick Mackey and Tony Reddan, it was a time of epic games involving the Glen, the

Barrs, Blackrock and Sarsfields because Cork city was the centre of hurling, long before the demographics changed and commuter towns developed.

My father introduced me to hurling and sport in general and did everything as it should be done in all aspects of his life. He was a fit man and because of that and his age, the possibility of illness never really crossed my mind. In fact the only time I remember something wrong with him occurred when he was bitten by what we thought was a Portuguese Man o' War jellyfish on holidays in Ardmore. He was swimming and was bitten on the bottom. We thought it was hilarious but there was an ambulance called and he spent two weeks in hospital on his stomach as it turned out to be quite serious.

But eventually age and illness did catch up with him and after working his way through the years as best and diligently as he could, and deserving of a good retirement where he could finally enjoy all the things he missed out on during hours in an office, he had a heart attack about six months before his working time was up. He had several more heart warnings through the 10 years he lived after retirement and it changed him. Before that he was a great gardener and very proud of his flowers and he'd have done a lot of walking. He was active so his life was completely restricted by his heart and what he loved doing was limited if not taken away from him. His final years were spoiled completely and that made the dark-haired boy think that life isn't fair sometimes.

I remember my mother as well and particularly her intelligence. She was a strong woman without being too intrusive. She had to be because she was a full-time housewife raising six children on practically no money. And to look back on it now, it was a family that was very anonymous and ordinary and didn't stand out for any reason. We had middle-class status but there was little income in the early stage of my parents' marriage. We were respectably poor so to speak but as children we never suffered shortages. That was probably because our parents suffered shortages that we never saw but growing up wasn't in any way lavish and didn't need to be.

In that way, my mother was the typical Irish mother. She somehow made ends meet and was strong in the sense she supported all her children and if we ever had any problems she was always there to help us out. In fact I consider myself to have had an extraordinary relationship with my mother. At one stage I had a girlfriend whose mother had no time for me. When you are in your late teens you can't understand what is wrong with you and why someone would take such a dislike to you. I had no difficulty in talking that through with my mother which I know was and is unusual but she calmed me down, gave me great advice because she knew this woman and gave me real insight on the background. It turned out that it was as simple as this woman not wanting to lose her daughter to any boy. That would never have entered my mind without the good counsel of my mother but in the end that remarkable closeness to her made her death harder to take than my father's.

We lived next door to the O'Learys and we were all very friendly and very close and did a lot of things together. My grandfather John Horgan had a plumbing and heating business and he had this big van that would take his workers to jobs wherever they were. We got a loan of this one Sunday and I remember 17 of us O'Herlihys and O'Learys were packed inside in it. We went to Ardmore and while that was a day-trip, our summer holidays were always for the entire month of June. We went usually to Myrtleville as kids and later to Ballycotton where there was a huge and beautiful house and all our friends would come to visit. Life and happiness would be packed inside the walls and I have no doubt our parents did without a lot to make sure we always had that summer break too.

They were the kinds of sacrifices they made, most of which I never knew, especially involving my father, until much later on. In those early days he didn't have a car and little wonder. He was a down-the-line clerk and while he'd have had a permanent and pensionable job, that didn't translate to income. But on Friday evenings he always came home with a present for us - and this was a measure of the man and his love for us - he could only afford it because he'd walk home. That way he could save the bus fare to get us something small, usually sweets. In fact when we were kids there was a great competition in our house to get the first kiss from Dad, and we'd be running to the bus stop each evening. That was the real O'Herlihy house, not the Sacred Heart version.

****

The voices of Dunphy and Brady and Giles discussing the game ahead bring me back for a moment to Studio Four, and the first ad break of the evening sweeps by. Finally the lads settle on how they'll tell the country how they think the next couple of hours will pan out.

There's a voice in my ear as well, telling me the ad break is coming to a close and there's a countdown once more. Dunphy is playing up his need for face time with a straight face though we all know by now this is a re-occurring joke. "Are the teams in the tunnel?" I ask upstairs. "Okay, they are in the tunnel. No more analysis. Just predictions lads." "Ah, those clips are important, but not that important I suppose," adds Dunphy as the floor manager, Ciarán McDonough, cuts in with time cues. The panel relax, settle down, and are ready for action.

Coming back in three... Three seconds for me to remember that boy and his one and only ambition in life, right through his school days.

That ambition was to be a journalist. Maybe it was built into my genes and I had a sense of continuity within me as there was a lot of journalism in my grandfather's family. It skipped a generation in the sense that my father was never interested but my grandfather was news editor of the Cork Examiner and my granduncles were journalists too - in Dublin in the Irish Press and in London with the Press Association. I wanted to be just like them but to even get that far in those days, you had to come through a lot.

Primary school was Glasheen National and I was a left hander. Ms Murphy was our teacher in high infants and first class and she was a very good woman with absolutely no cruelty attached to her. But she believed, as everyone did at the time, you should only use your right hand when writing. So my left hand was tied behind my back and I was compelled to use my right. It was amazing how it confused me. In fact if I hadn't been a Catholic and didn't bless myself with my right, my brain was so puzzled by what was being forced on me, I wouldn't have had a clue which way was which. And for many years afterwards, because of that, I couldn't instantly tell left from right. Research into left handers forced to use their right says a lot of people contracted a stammer as a result but, thankfully, it just left me baffled for a few years.

It was a small school at that stage and we got a temporary teacher, Mr Holly. And Ms Murphy had us pray every morning that we'd get enough students so he could become permanent. Joe Holly ended up as headmaster because there was a population explosion in the western suburbs soon after but I finished up there at a young age and I went straight on to

St Finbarr's College in Farranferris and straight into second year. If I had no problems with Glasheen, I could never say the same about where I spent many of my teenage days.

Farranferris was a minor diocesan seminary and if you wanted to be a priest in the Cork Diocese you had to go there on your journey to Maynooth. I'd no interest in being a priest although some of my relations did. My first cousin Paddy O'Leary had every intention and because he went there, so did I as we were born within a day of each other, lived next door to each other and were great friends. There were only 18 day pupils in my time in Farranferris, the rest were boarders primarily from west Cork, so it was a mix and match of kids with various mindsets. We had some very good teachers too, including John A Murphy who taught us history and English. He was the only lay teacher there at the time and went on to become a Senator and had a major role in UCC.

It was a very unsophisticated school in many ways but the standard of teaching was very good and there was no problem with any teacher there except a man called Dr Dan Connolly who all of us juniors thought at the time was a sadist. He is a long time dead now, but he was one of those priests who never wanted to be a teacher, he wanted to be a pastoral priest and resented being assigned to Farranferris. Somehow he went on to become President of the college and ultimately a Canon in St Peter and Paul's Church in the centre of Cork city. But when we were young he used to terrorise us. I'm not exaggerating – there is no other way to describe our first year. But I must make one thing clear, he was the exception. No other teacher behaved as he did and in fact there was generally a very good relationship between the teachers and the boys. But Connolly made our lives a misery in Junior 2.

We called him Texas Dan and each day we had him for the

opening classes, first Greek followed by Latin. I remember one day doing Greek, and as the class came to the end he said, "Tomorrow gentlemen we'll be doing the Greek numerals and whatever numeral you miss, you'll be punished". The next day I was asked the Greek for the numeral 47, I didn't know it and his punishment was 47 slaps across the face - and one slap had two parts, one to each cheek. He packed up before reaching his target but even so he was well into the double figures and had made his point.

He was worse to others in our class though. I remember a boy called Jim Keating from Crosshaven, a lovely guy who was most unfortunate because he came to school each day by bus and the bus schedule meant he could never arrive for nine o'clock. He was always a couple of minutes late for Greek. He'd run the last couple of hundred yards up the hill to the school and arrive panting into the classroom. The second he got in the door, he was asked a question. Immediately. No chance to settle. Not surprisingly, he never had the answer and always had an excuse. He knew he was going to be asked a question and he was completely flummoxed on the grounds that he was in turmoil mentally and physically from his run. I don't know how he hung in there.

Wearing his soutane, Connolly used to occasionally sit on the storage heaters in the depths of winter. One particular morning he said to the partly-disoriented Keating, "Come here to me Jim". So he sat him down next to him and Connolly put one arm around him and one on his knee and said, "Jim, why is it that every single time that I ask you a question, you never know the answer? And you always give me some kind of an excuse? Why don't you simply say that you don't know?"

"Well you never give me a chance," was the response and we didn't realise until he said it, but his leg was pinned down hard and in those days we wore shortpants to junior school. "Father, you are burning my leg on the heater," Jim said but Connolly kept on talking and kept his leg pressed down. Eventually he stopped and let Jim go to his desk. Today Connolly could possibly get jail for what was by any measurement an assault.

Connolly was terrifying as well because we never knew where he stood and there was a fella called Paud Murphy who he accused of telling a lie one time and got stuck into this about 10 minutes before the end of our first class. Paud was a very good hurler and kept saying he wasn't telling a lie and he wouldn't admit anything because he hadn't done anything wrong. But Connolly was lashing his hand with a stick and then went out, saying he'd be back shortly for the next class. The tension among the young boys was unbelievable. We just sat there waiting and didn't know what would happen when he returned. Would he continue the punishment? Would he come back and do worse? In the end he came back in and just ignored the whole thing. It was over in his mind but as kids that aspect was mentally exhausting.

By the time we got to the Leaving Honours class for Latin, the sadism we experienced in our early days had gone because Connolly was a different person. Maybe he knew he was moving on or maybe he had come to terms with the fact he wasn't going to move out of the place. But he was certainly a different person except for this one incident. He said to the Latin class, "Now gentlemen, we come to the word deceit. I want you to tell me what can you do with 'deceit'." Paddy O'Leary piped up. "Well you can sit on the seat, Father." Connolly did not appreciate the humour and beat lumps out of him.

But that man was capable of more than physical cruelty. He was very ungenerous, particularly to Paddy, who was very bright, much more so than me. He got a hiding on one of our early days in school and his father went up to Connolly and told him if he ever put a finger on his son, or any one of his sons who would go through the school, he'd go to the Bishop and if necessary the Gardaí. But Paddy's father died soon after and the family would've lived on whatever pension he had from Eustace - the builders suppliers in Cork city and I can only imagine it would have been hugely limited.

Paddy wanted to be a priest but his mother said he'd have to start earning for a while first and he accepted that. So he was offered a job in the Scottish Union Insurance Company, provided he got a very good Leaving Cert and a very good reference. And Paddy got the Leaving Cert honours no problem but when he went to Connolly, who was President at that stage, for a reference, he wouldn't give it to him. His excuse was he gave a reference to someone else for that job and couldn't give two references for the same job. None of us believed a word of it and we were absolutely certain it was his way of getting back at the family because he'd been challenged by Paddy's father.

I saw Connolly years later when he was Parish Priest and took huge pleasure in walking straight past him. But when I was talking to other fellas who were in other schools I realised they wouldn't put up with that. We let a huge amount go, as did our parents, because Connolly was a priest. Priests had a special place in society when I was a boy, they were rarely challenged and Connolly took advantage of it. Without a collar he would not have got away with it as I know from pals in other schools who were not slow to hit back if they felt they were being assaulted.

But if other priests in that place weren't violent, some were certainly odd. There was another priest there, Fr McCarthy, who was in charge of the hurling team. My brother Jack was a super hurler who played for the Cork minors but he went on what we call the lang in Cork - mitching to people from elsewhere - for about six weeks. Yet he still played every Wednesday for Farranferris. He'd just turn up for the matches. One week he came along for a game and Fr McCarthy said, "Now listen Jack, I'm telling you this, if we don't win this match today, just be aware of one thing. I will tell your father you are not going to school". Can you imagine that. Fr McCarthy was passionate about hurling and Farranferris had a good team with the Harty Cup in their sights but what a distorted sense of priorities for a man who went on to become Parish Priest of Ballincollig. Farna won that particular game, McCarthy said nothing to Dad but Jack was eventually caught by his Irish teacher who turned him in.

Farranferris was a fee-paying school and although there wasn't much money involved, it was an awful lot for Dad and when word got home that Jack was on the lang, my mother was scandalised and sent Jack to his bedroom. She said, "Your father will deal with you when he comes home". I'll never forget the tension as we awaited Dad's return from work and when he got back he was told the full story and he was appalled. He had an old fashioned cut-throat razor that had to be sharpened each day with a strap before he used it. He went to the bathroom, took the strap and gave Jack a few lashes with his trousers down. We were pleading with him not to do it but his argument was he was working bloody hard, he didn't have much money, he'd put it into education and it wasn't for his children to go on the lang for six weeks. So Jack got what my father used to call his lamb and salad. He'd done wrong and was punished but that was the end of it then.

"And in two," continues Ciarán the floor manager. Two seconds for me to remember that boy and his meeting in the

newspaper.

By the time I was 15 I'd had enough of Connolly and that school. Besides, I had got my Matric, and at that stage it was a tougher exam than the Leaving Cert. The Matric was the entry into university but I was too young as you had to wait until you were 18 to enter third level. So, instead of hanging around in school for a few more years, I wanted out and explored whether or not it would be possible to become a journalist in the Cork Examiner. And whatever about journalism being in my genes, getting a meeting certainly was because one day my father brought me down to their offices and we met with Tom Crosbie, Chairman of the Examiner.

The Crosbies would have been among the aristocrats of Cork society and they were good people, good employers, paternalistic and loyal to the families who worked for them. Tom Crosbie was a remote figure to most of us but when Dad made contact and asked him to see us he immediately said yes. The door was wide open. That was the only time I met him. I thought he was very warm and I suspect in the great paternalistic tradition of the paper perhaps he thought I could be one of another generation of O'Herlihys who could make a contribution.

Our meeting was brief, no more than 15 minutes but it was very pleasant. I kept quiet and Tom Crosbie spent the bulk of the time reminiscing with my father about my grandfather Willie O'Herlihy. Then he turned to me and said, "I want to say something to you, young Willie," as he called me. "Any O'Herlihy is good enough for the Examiner. Your grandfather was a wonderful news editor and there's a great pedigree of journalism in your family. Now we don't have a job for you at this minute but as soon as there is one available, we'll let you know."

I walked away from the meeting, impatient at no instant

job, my feelings a bizarre cocktail of excitement and disappointment. I went back to school wondering if I'd ever get my chance but about two months before the Leaving Cert, I got a letter from the Examiner saying there was a job in the Reading Room which was mine if I wanted it but I had to let them know immediately. I didn't have to think twice about it although my mother was appalled. It was the height of madness in her mind that I would take a job instead of doing my Leaving Cert. But she also knew there was no stopping me from taking my chance to go into the newspaper business. I started 10 days later.

The Reading Room doesn't exist anymore, but when journalists' copy was subbed it went to the printing floor, and just to make sure there were no mistakes one last time, it came back to the reading room. Every single drip of ink, including ads, was corrected and sent back to the printers. That was where all the Examiner journalists started in my time and where you learned to understand the culture and the style of the paper. It wasn't exhilarating but it was a start. So I felt fortunate to be in the door.

Granted, I had no money at the very beginning. I was reading about all the sports events, checking for mistakes all day long, but my first salary was two pounds and 10 shillings which in today's money equates to just over €2 per week. Then I got a massive increase of 15 shillings and thought I was the king. I could go to the movies, have a date, give money to my mother, which perhaps helped soothe her annoyance and still have change left over. But I had no money for a car or anything and in the years that followed I'd get markings and have to go to Riverstown or Coachford for matches and if the bus times didn't suit, I'd cycle. Later on in life I was talking to a reporter in the Irish Times and he told me that when he was in the Clare Champion he had a cycling allowance. If only I'd known.

"And in one," finishes Ciarán the floor manager, interrupting my stream of thoughts yet again. One second for me to remember the boy and his early days in the newspaper game.

I worked in that Reading Room for about eight months although at that age is seemed a lifetime. But slowly I came out of my shell and can remember having a big row with a senior person there. There was a columnist called Eden - his real name was Paddy Kelly who was a former editor of the Cork Examiner and he was talking about the Antarctic. He wrote that "it was nothing but miles and miles of nothing but miles and miles". This more senior reader was adamant that it was a mistake, that he really meant "it was nothing but miles and miles" which was to miss the entire point of the sentence and I was trying to explain this. It got heated and it was only after that altercation that I realised this guy had no idea what he was talking about and had no concept of journalism. To him it was just a pay cheque and when I lost that argument I was disgusted.

Eventually I was transferred to the Commercial Department and was in charge of sales of the Cork Evening Echo. I did that for two months and hated every minute of it. I had to check the sales going out each evening, balance the cash and do the kind of jobs that I never saw as a part of journalism and I felt they weren't bringing me any closer to my goal of being a reporter. But finally, from there I was transferred to the Echo editorial and I was a sub-editor well before I was 17.

It is hard to imagine now but everything was very structured and ordered and people even went home to lunch. Because of that, I found myself in a situation that the vast percentage of the copy came in during that time and there was no one there but me. It was a crazy set up given the fact

I was just a kid and there were absolutely masses of stories arriving with just me to deal with.

Initially, I simply organised everything so that when the editor came back I would say, "Mr O'Connell, there are five things I think might make a lead story". His full name was William Declan O'Connell, a very nice man but given my age and position, he was daunting. He was a forbidding type of guy, was tall, had a moustache, smoked a pipe and took himself very seriously. And he was intimidating for a number of reasons. Firstly, because if you worked for him you were expected to do your job and be good enough to do it well. And secondly, he was intolerant if you made a mess of something.

In every way, he was an old-fashioned Editor, and carried himself in a distant and high-powered way. I was the serf but if he had rows they weren't with me because I was either too small or insignificant and was expected to know my place. He called me Willie as well and more and more I noticed as he headed out at midday, he'd say, "Every time I come back from my lunch, I want you to have the lead story waiting for me on my desk". It showed he was gaining confidence in me but it brought its own pressure. But once everyone had left the building for an hour, there was a relief too because I was my own man and didn't feel as though I was being watched.

One day, and the Echo never knew this of course, there was no lead story. Nothing that I could justify making the front page. It was before the war in Vietnam, or Indochina as it was then, but there was a huge battle that was symbolic and important in terms of everything that followed. It was in Dien Bien Phu, and I got a paragraph in over the wires and decided this would be fine as long as I could spice it up a little. I justified this to myself by saying in my head the readers of the Echo don't give a damn about Indochina. Perhaps

I was in a little bit of a panic but I had to improvise too so I got my typewriter and fabricated an entire story based on this paragraph. There was hand-to-hand fighting and all kinds of stuff going on by the time I was finished with it. When the Editor came back, he said "Willie, have you got my lead". "There you go," I said hoping he wouldn't see what had been done. And as it turns out he didn't and it led the Echo that night. It passed the editor and the readers and none were any the wiser.

I worked in the Echo editorial for about four years, but a part of me at that stage also had an interest in studying law. I had to decide whether I wanted to become a reporter, or stay forever as a sub-editor, because the latter job could have easily accommodated a night degree. Thankfully I decided against law on the grounds that I felt if I committed four years to becoming a lawyer, I'd never progress as a journalist. I stuck with it, and finally I got the opportunity of going into the news room where, in those days, you could end up writing anything from murders to court cases and even, in my case, a social column.

I took it very seriously, too much so for my age, and was appalled on one occasion in the District Court when I was approached by a man and asked to keep his name out of the paper. He was up on a drink driving charge and he offered me 10 shillings. I walked away exuding integrity and thinking this was a big deal, while all the time trying to climb the ladder and become Editor of the Examiner. That was what I wanted from life and I never had any intention of leaving that newspaper or that city. Why would I? I was and am an immensely tribal Corkman and the Examiner had very good reporters and they were terrific employers. I loved the whole atmosphere of the place and there was a great sense of the senior reporters helping the younger people out.

Take Tom Barker, who was one of the specialist Court reporters who used to take over the news desk when the news
editor was on holidays. Usually he was down to earth but
when he stepped up, he took his temporary role very seriously and if he recognised you wrote well or had potential,
he assisted you hugely. He was in charge one time when I
had to do a story on Charlie Chaplin coming through Cork
Airport. We got the arrival time wrong and when I got there
he had come and gone on his way to Kerry but I chatted
to people who had seen, met or talked to him and wrote a
colour story and it appeared the following day. Barker said,
"Well Bill, that was a very good story but I didn't like the
way you split an infinitive". "Mr Barker," I replied, "I have
no idea in the wide world how to split an infinitive". So he
explained it and from that day through to today, I never did
it again.

I dabbled in sports writing as well, not because they saw me
as any expert but more out of necessity. I had played hurling
and football at junior level and played soccer for Crofton
Celtic as a schoolboy. But no matter how good I might have
been my playing career never progressed because I was reporting on Saturdays and Sundays from the time I was 16. I
knew if I wanted to make it in the Examiner, a sacrifice had
to be made. Only Val Dorgan could have gotten away with
both worlds existing together because he was hurling for
Glen Rovers and Cork. On top of that, in my estimation he
was the best journalist of his generation in the country. He
was a magnificent Gaelic games reporter, a terrific news reporter, and had the capacity to write every style be it for the
Daily Mirror or the London Times.

He'd a fantastic range of writing skills. In time he became
Europe correspondent of the paper and there is a picture of
himself and John Healy, hugely emotional, watching Ire-

land in the penalty shoot-out against Romania in Genoa in 1990 when a Euro Summit in Dublin was suspended to see the climax of the game. We would have been competitors as young reporters but we were good friends. Over time I wrote on hurling, football and strangely enough hockey. Eventually soccer came into the equation too.

But that soccer reporting was so far from this studio and these famous names beside me and this game tonight. When I did my first FAI Cup match in Dalymount Park, I found the Examiner was at the very back of the press seats, with every freelance operator. All the other daily papers were right up the front. I said this to Joe Wickham, then-General Secretary of the FAI. "I'm not putting up with this, we are a daily paper, not some Mickey Mouse paper or some provincial paper." So we were brought to the very front. I felt the status of the Examiner, which I was very proud of, was being undermined and I made the protest on principle.

If I was branching out in terms of sports, I was branching out in terms of the media as well. I began with radio - Junior Sports Magazine with Harry Thullier and Jimmy Magee. Bill Twomey, manager of the Cork Opera House, was their man in the city but he was also a rugby commentator. When he was on provincial and international duty I stood in for him and eventually they asked me to work with them every week. I was delighted. I loved radio, loved the immediacy of it, loved the buzz it gave me and again I was lucky. Fred Cogley was reorganising RTÉ's radio coverage and he asked me to work out of Cork for them each weekend. Fred was a terrific friend and mentor and I owe him so much but he wasn't above giving me a bollocking when I deserved it.

I was essentially a reporter but one Sunday Fred asked me to do a League of Ireland game at Turner's Cross in Cork as a commentator and frankly, I blew it. My commentary was awful and at half-time Fred gave it to me in the neck. "You're boring the listeners to death" he told me. "But the game is terrible," I said, "nothing is happening." "I don't care", said Fred, "lift it, give the impression something will happen".

I decided after that I wasn't going to be a commentator, and I'd say they decided the same thing. But that was only a small setback and in 1965 I did my first television interview. That was one of those moments I never saw coming around the bend. Television was never in my plans, never once considered, because I never thought of myself as having the voice, the looks, the talent or the charisma to work on television. In fact I was pretty sure that I didn't have any of those things and wouldn't have the ability to make it on television.

But with that thought in my head, the floor manager's countdown ends and we are back from the break. And through the lens of the camera, I talk to the television audience just as I've been doing for what seems a lifetime.

CHAPTER 2

Start Spreading The News

If so much of what will be said on this show tonight is different, so much of what happens off air remains the same. That's just the way everyone around here likes it. Take Giles and Brady and Dunphy in the studio. In that order, it's how they always take their seats in relation to me and even at the pre-show meeting a minute's walk from here in Studio Four, they have their individual corners of the office table and no-one takes their spot. It's just easier that way. But it's not solely those simple routines that remain the same either. Take the lads' characters as well. They, too, remain constant and they are very predictable in their mannerisms away from camera. And over the years I like to think I have worked them out and know each of them inside out.

"Right lads, what way is tonight likely to pan out and briefly, because we are out of time, your prediction on who is going to win," I ask them. So, they make their predictions that they've been mulling over since we all got together. "We shall see," I add, "so let's hand over to our commentary team of Ray Houghton, and first, George Hamilton". With that, the atmosphere in the room changes as the small red light on top of camera number two blinks out and the place comes back to life. The runners bring tea and coffee. The make-up girl who will spend ad breaks doing touch-ups or make up checks departs for 45 minutes. Cameramen, sound engineers, the autocue operator and studio crew begin talking and moving about. Studio Four is restored to life after television – for the moment.

There's nothing special about this, it's always like this on match days. It's life as we know it between live television inserts. We relax and I glance at John Giles who sits nearest me. I think for the thousandth time how decent he is, how shrewd and clever he is and that's unusual because time has shown that those who were intelligent footballers don't necessarily become intelligent and successful people in other areas of their lives, particularly when it comes to punditry.

In fact, Giles has made that claim to me many times and I remember that he refused to take part any further in Sky's 'The Footballer's Football Show' because he felt the other panellists, all international footballers, did not know what they were talking about and he wasn't prepared in that circumstance to be part of the show. However Giles to my mind has been the opposite in his transition from player to pundit. He bucked the trend and he has achieved huge respect here and among UK media for his soccer analysis. He is very secure in his views, not just on soccer, but a subject that fascinated him - socialism in politics. One of the many fascinating discussions we have off-air in studio is the change in Britain brought about by Margaret Thatcher and the damage she did to their sense of community. He cannot abide her legacy and is very clinical in picking apart that legacy.

John is strong, logical and convincing in his views and people rarely win an argument with him on his soccer opinions. Brady and Dunphy aren't joking when they call him the senior analyst and it is fascinating to listen to the inter-play between them in the 90-minute meeting we have before this and every programme. His views command huge respect and you must know and stand your ground if you challenge him. Over a long career as a player and a manager, Giles has earned his respect and the panel reflect this in their attitude to him.

So do I because he is a very good friend and he'd always give you a hand. What I liked about Giles when we started broadcasting together was that he never once patronised me and never tried to talk down to me or show me up despite his far superior knowledge of the game. And he could have easily arrived with an attitude problem because when he began working with us on the 1986 World Cup he wasn't wanted by RTÉ Sport. They were so reluctant to get him on board that Dunphy had a huge job in trying to convince the Sports Department of his qualities. He even threatened to walk off the show and away from the station if his demand for Giles to join wasn't met. That was the only way he felt he could win what he saw as a hugely important argument.

He wanted Giles on board because he came to the conclusion, and understandably so, that during our time together, a full eight years, we had nearly talked ourselves out. We were on for entire matches with no commercial breaks and inevitably we were beginning to repeat ourselves. Of course Dunphy was right even if some people saw it as an old pals act as he and Giles were close friends and had worked together at Shamrock Rovers.

Dunphy often talks about the times before Giles when there had been just the two of us on the show. From the 1978 World Cup through the 1980 European Championships and 1982 World Cup and on into the 1984 European Championships. And it was there that Dunphy overreached. Michel Platini became a target with Dunphy saying he hadn't the bottle even though he scored seven goals as France came through the group stage without a nick. Giles had

actually played against Platini twice and one of those times
was a 1-0 victory in Dublin on a muddy and windy day. He'd
noted that Platini simply didn't show up and Dunphy probably read too much into that remark, as, on a Sunday evening
before we handed over to Marseille for the European semi-
final, he said Platini would be shown up by Portugal.

"He's a good player but that's it. He's not the great player
everyone is making him out to be. There's a difference between a good and a great player and he doesn't fall into that
second category." But he then watched on as the Juventus
player got a winner in the last minute of extra-time and
France eventually went on to win that tournament on home
soil. He looked great to everyone watching.

Even at that stage, Dunphy confided in Giles. He actually
asked him straight out in private, "Am I wrong about this
fella Platini?". "No you are not wrong," answered Giles, "but
you are mad to be saying it so strongly on television". Dunphy knew well at that stage who he needed as a partner and
he kept up his campaign to persuade Tim O'Connor and
Mike Horgan, the two who controlled soccer on television,
to let Giles onto the show but they were not budging.

Dunphy felt he was out of road as a solo artist and he
needed another analyst to counterbalance his forthright
opinions. The hierarchy got that much but they didn't want
Giles because of how his media performances had been
throughout his management career. In their view, Giles was
very conservative in his attitude to the media, he would
never attack players and would always give the minimum
possible to papers and television in his managerial roles. He
was considered to have nothing to say.

Nothing could be further from the truth and the reality
was, as Giles explained to us later, as manager he never felt it
was his place to blabber to journalists about his players. His

thinking was that if he said something as simple as the midfield was problematic, it would be interpreted in a way that meant he was having a go at those players. For that reason he was extra cautious and he'd tell you himself that he would have been a bit of a nightmare for those running the show. Football was interesting in his mind in that the job of the media was to get as much from a manager while the job of a manager was to give as little to the media. For that reason he wasn't popular with many.

It wasn't that there was hostility towards him as a person either because Giles is a very nice person and everyone was very aware of that. But the hostility was on the grounds of putting someone who would say nothing and was boring onto a programme that prided itself on saying something and being entertaining. In their view it could have ruined everything Dunphy and I had striven to create.

Yet, despite that, Dunphy continued to talk of Giles as an icon who had a very special place in sport in Ireland. Again he told Tim of his regard for Giles, how the show had gone stale and suggested that Giles should come on board as soon as possible. Again the answer was a swift and firm no. Giles the manager had been notoriously monosyllabic with the press and he didn't like journalists and wasn't a good communicator. But Dunphy stuck to his guns and brought me into the argument.

I didn't know Giles personally and he didn't know me at all. He would have done the occasional interview with me when he was over Ireland but that was it. Also, when myself and Dunphy were on air for the 1978 World Cup, Giles was in America. Four years later, he was in Canada. He wouldn't have seen me broadcast at all but that didn't bother Dunphy as he'd his mind set on this. "You would bring the best out in him and get him talking, Bill," he told me. "We have to make this happen." And finally, with Dunphy possibly heading for the door, RTÉ agreed to give Giles his chance, but with a great deal of reluctance.

Giles knew all that and for the World Cup in Mexico, he initially took the view that his arrival on the panel was like a month's holidays. He saw his first contribution to the show as simply a one-off with no long-term future for him so it didn't matter how good or bad he was. For that reason, he took it very casually because it was obvious in his mind that he wouldn't be there come the following season. He had no commitment in the English League at the time so it was something to occupy him for a couple of weeks. Some might say it was courageous to come into an environment where you aren't wanted but Giles was and is as tough as nails. He showed that in his career as a player and very quickly he started to show that to RTÉ during the World Cup as he grew into the role. People saw the real Giles with an unparalleled knowledge of the game and made himself an unmissable and permanent fixture thereafter.

When he and I got chatting all those years ago, he quickly recognised my deficiencies, and tried to round off my knowledge. He has always been to me something of a mentor and I've learned an awful lot from him and he's always gone out of his way to show me how things work in football. He would show me guys who hide in matches and this kind of thing and he has gotten great pleasure in showing me some of the nuances of the game that I wouldn't have immediately recognised. My knowledge of the game is infinitely bigger than it was and it's largely because I learned from him.

And for all that, from the very beginning, I've had huge time for him and now he sits beside me, awaiting the kick off anxiously, in the hope that all the study he's done for the match tonight pays off and he's proven right yet again.

START SPREADING THE NEWS

Finally he turns to me and points out aspects of the tactical game that will play out, aspects that never even crossed my mind, and as always I find it fascinating. "You see this guy Bill, if they can get him the ball in those wide areas and release him early, they'll do some serious damage and here is why." I scribble his words on my notepad for reference and use if appropriate.

People may think it's odd that I hold Dunphy in a similar regard considering how different they are. He is furthest from me in studio now, and as I put my pen down and look up again, he is pulling in a chair for the floor manager to watch the game but his gesture is matched by strong words. "Sit in there and don't be scared of me. Hey, by the way, it's freezing in here, can we do something about the heating," he shouts out as his homemade curry prepared by his wife Jane appears on the desk to be consumed during the opening 45 minutes. "Is anyone listening? Can we put on the heating."

He is volatile and everyone knows it. He can blow up on issues I'd regard not worth getting stressed about, never mind erupting over. He gets ridiculously passionate about matters others may consider minor. It's not an insecurity though, nor a lack of self-control. Indeed I think it's a great strength. In terms of any sports panel in RTÉ, Dunphy has had the strongest influence on the success of the concept and the proof, if needed, is that there is nearly always a Dunphy-type figure on panels for other games.

Our formula has transferred in more recent years to rugby and GAA coverage because what we do in soccer is so good, and works so well. George Hook, Pat Spillane and Joe Brolly are the Dunphy-like figures in the other main sports, but as they say in the classics "there's only one Eamon Dunphy".

Yet Dunphy is still out on his own and one good thing about him is that he can laugh at himself. At the extravagant attitude he sometimes postulates, at the satirical comments of Aprés Match, at his good humoured demand for face time, at the letters that are sometimes anything but complimentary and at the suggestion he is now a moderate and no longer the radical of old. Tonight, though, it's agitated.

"It's still cold," he barks again, unimpressed by the lack of an immediate improvement in temperature. Some jump at his words but this is a matter for the floor manager. Giles and Brady have other matters to occupy them as a television on wheels is pulled closer so the panel can watch the game and form their opinions for half-time. And as I look across at the three of them and their vastly differing yet predictable mannerisms, I sometimes feel the four of us are like a small repertory company who know our roles though the lines change regularly.

****

If the lads have their own routines then so do I. At 4.30pm on match days I arrive into the Television Centre, greet the receptionists and it's out with my pass, through the doors, down the stairs, along the corridor that leads into wardrobe. Or at least it used to be called that when I started out. Earlier today, for the first time, I noticed the sign on the door read 'costume department'.

Surrounded by rows and rows of any and every type of clothing, I'm asked what colour shirt I'd like. I went with white and one was chosen from a selection of suits and jackets they keep just for me. "What colour handkerchief would you like to go with the jacket," I'm asked. "Whatever is the most appropriate", I say. Yellow is produced.

Taking my jacket and white shirt and yellow handkerchief I passed some clothes marked 'Graeme Souness' and an entire

rail marked 'Glas Vegas' and headed for the changing rooms.
There I put on the cable to which they attach the mic under
the shirt and jacket while leaving on the jeans I arrived in.
Nobody can see them at home anyway and it's more comfortable this way. It was all very relaxed, just as it is every day
I come to the RTÉ Studios. When I look back, though, there
was nothing relaxed about my introduction to television.

I remember when I was new to this business. Pat Smiley of
the Irish Times and I both happened to be working at the
Cork Show. People knew me from television and he said to
me quite seriously, "My God, if I was on television like you,
I'd really cash in". He was talking about women obviously
but he didn't know what it was like for a callow youth lack-
ing in confidence and sophistication. When we went into the
towns and villages of Ireland hundreds would watch us work
and I'd hear the comments of the women saying things like,
"My God, he's smaller than I thought he was," or "He's not
good looking at all, how do they put him on the television".
So instead of basking in fame and imagining I was an up-
and-coming television star, I started to shrink into myself.
Back then, just as now I suppose, many who were on the box
had massive confidence and some had big egos too.

Their jobs imbued them with a self-importance I couldn't
comprehend or replicate. I was terrified a lot of the time and
there was no question of me "cashing in" as Smiley put it. I
was just trying to get by without making a fool of myself. In
saying that and despite having to carry myself with a confidence I never naturally had, it was a great time to be on
television in a lot of ways because it was a new and exciting
medium and we were learning as we went along.

In my early days on television I still worked in the Examiner and I found myself writing more and more about soccer
not just for my own paper but as stringer for every paper that

required the service, from the Irish Times to the Irish Independent to the Press to the Express to the Mirror. This was agreed with the Examiner and there was no difficulty as long as I didn't short-change my employers and kept the best stuff for them. Getting other papers' employees to give you a dig out wasn't uncommon and RTÉ were about to take advantage of that working practice as well.

At that stage Roy Hammond was the main cameraman in Cork for television news while Joe McCarthy was trying his best to become the features cameraman. Joe succeeded because he had flair, determination and persistence and he would go on to have a huge influence on my career. But in the first instance, it was Roy who was approached by Frank Hall and the Newsbeat team in RTÉ. They wanted to do a story on the 50th anniversary of the sinking of the Lusitania liner which was torpedoed off Kinsale by a German U-boat during the First World War. And they wanted Roy to get somebody to interview a survivor.

Newsbeat's focus was essentially provincial Ireland and was very much the Nationwide of its day. It was very popular because of Frank Hall's style which was humorous, offbeat, sardonic and appealed hugely to the audience of the day. He was one of the great stars of the early days of television and I sometimes felt he was not fully appreciated for the quality and range of his output. Later, Hall's Pictorial Weekly was groundbreaking and I marvelled at his output - week in, week out for some 26 weeks a year. By today's measurement and practice that was phenomenal.

But back to Newsbeat. This particular edition needed two presenters from the south. Paddy McCarthy, who worked for the Cork office of the Irish Independent which he joined from the New Hartford Times in the US where he did some TV work, was sent to the Old Head of Kinsale. There he did a scene set on the story – "Behind me the Lusitania had set sail for America and just a few miles from here was torpe-doed etc etc" His function was to lay out the facts and to set up the story.

My role was very different as I was asked to go to Cappo-quin to meet this survivor who was in the local hospital. Roy thought of me when the request came down from Dublin but it took him three days to convince me to do it because I didn't think I had the voice, the appearance or the pres-ence. And I certainly had no interest in television because my focus always was on becoming the editor of the Exam-iner. Eventually though I said yes, with one proviso - use it if it's good enough but bin it if it's not. I had no experience in television and I wanted to be saved national embarrassment. This was agreed but at the same time I thought, "It's a one-off, let's give it a go. I still have my typewriter and my job in the Examiner".

So off to Cappoquin to meet the woman for the interview. Within seconds I was even more sure my life would be in the Examiner and behind that typewriter. God help her and me, she was lovely, helpful, half-senile and naturally, as a result, the interview was awful. Really atrocious. We had to do a few takes to even get something that was semi-acceptable. It was like getting blood out of a stone and she just couldn't get the words out. She was cooperative but she didn't have much to stay at that stage of her life and I was actually nervous sending the report back for the programme team because I knew what the reaction would be. Yet somehow it was used and Frank Hall gave an instruction that I was to do all the work out of Cork. He saw something in me and continued long after that to see something in me that I never saw in myself.

As for Joe McCarthy, he had the capacity to see way be-

39

yond hard news and he could tell there were untapped stories available out of Cork and the south that nobody was exploiting. Newsbeat, a news features programme, was the obvious platform. They recognised it wasn't properly servicing the regions because of budget and manpower limitations. So Joe made a powerful argument to supply stories on a weekly basis. Frank Hall and Dick Hill who ran the programme gave the go ahead and Joe and I began a long and fruitful working relationship. The untapped stories that Joe had recognised became our meat and drink.

In the early days of our relationship, it was very much the blind leading the blind as he had no more concept of the dynamics and mechanics of television than I had. But slowly we grew and in an era where so much was repetitive, he was a guy who thought carefully and visually about the work we were doing and I came to rely hugely on him. He was in effect the director and for about three years he and I worked comfortably together and grew in confidence and understanding of the medium.

If there was a special moment in our working relationship it came in Cobh. We were halfway through a story when I said to Joe, "This isn't good television. We've got to change and broaden the visuals". We took time out, re-examined every element from a visual viewpoint and re-shot the story with more colour, more supportive shots and in effect began a process that continued all through our work together. We had to be careful though because, hard to imagine now, but we worked on film, com mag or sep mag and that was very different to video. You couldn't do take after take and waste film and if you did Newsbeat gave you a bollocking for wasting film which was expensive.

But for the most part Frank Hall and his team were happy. I was still working in the Examiner, so Joe was the person who would interact with the show and tell them here were three very good stories we could do that week. We'd get approval and off we'd go and deliver. A couple of times they wanted to see me in Dublin to talk through things, and it was then I would meet Frank but for little more than short conversations. There was never any real guidance given about what we were doing and whether certain aspects were right or wrong or how we might improve, that wasn't the way television worked back then. You either sank or swam. In fact I never got any sort of formal training and looking back now, it showed in those 'Newsbeat' days.

I've no problem doing a live show like tonight and I enjoy a good performance that involves getting a strong reaction from Giles or Brady or Dunphy. I know what makes good television and what the viewers of this show want in terms of content and entertainment. But it was very different in the old days. Sometimes I'd catch a glimpse of 'Reeling in the Years' and see myself in early television stories and I feel like watching through my fingers. Some of what I was doing back then was so serious and intense, it looks like Monty Python. Amateurish might be a kind way to describe some of my work.

I started working on television in 1965 and did more and more throughout 1966. The Examiner had no problem as long as I did my own job. I was very careful about this because the Examiner was generous to me about my television work. They always got my stories before they were aired on Newsbeat so they were happy. So were Joe and myself because we were making progress but we were exhausted too because our three stories a week had to fit into the Examiner's schedule and we covered the country right up to Sligo. The pressure was huge, more so when we gained not just experience but the reputation for reliability.

Burt Budin, an American, was one of Newsbeat's producers and he'd regularly call to check up on the progress of our stories. Most of the time everything was fine but there was one occasion when we struggled to get what he wanted. We said down the line to him, "Look, we haven't the story for you because we haven't an important interview and it won't be good enough without it". He was having none of it. "I don't want it good," he said, "I want it Tuesday". It's a great line but he was deadly serious so we had to get it to him because they had committed on that Tuesday to a 10-minute piece from us and a daily programme has little luxury. That is what we called pressure.

Between Newsbeat and the Examiner I was working long hours and was flat out but I was young and I loved it. I used to work for RTÉ around my two days off a week and I usually worked in the paper at weekends because of sport. Other times I might be working from seven until three and then we'd start our 'Newsbeat' efforts. We always found a way and it didn't bother me in the least because it was enjoyable and stimulating and the Examiner didn't mind because it wasn't affecting them in any way. They were getting our stories and I suppose my getting my name out there was of some benefit to them.

The stories I did for Newsbeat weren't exactly hard nor did it require hours of research and fact-checking. There were features like the one I did with Tim Hayes, a harmless guy who buried himself alive for fame and in order to get into the Guinness Book of Records. There was Jayne Mansfield too, a ridiculous story that could only have taken place in the Ireland of that time.

She was Marilyn Monroe-lite, a sex symbol with huge boobs and the beguiling voice of an ingénue. She was touring a one-woman show and was contracted to play the Mount

Brandon Hotel in Tralee. The booking caused uproar. I doubt if many had seen her films and certainly no-one had seen her stage show but the conventional wisdom in Kerry was that if someone flaunted their sexuality like Jayne then they had to be immoral and her show was considered a possible occasion of sin for the boys of Tralee. Laughable now but not then because the Bishop and the priests got involved and exerted so much pressure on the community in those days.

Newsbeat instructed Joe and I to hotfoot it to Kerry but shortly after we got there the show was cancelled. The hotel bowed to the pressure. Mansfield decided to do a press conference, attended by about 50 journalists, mostly from the United Kingdom. I was the only television reporter there so I was told to start the conference questioning. I was just a young lad, this was a major international story, and I felt very much out of my depth. Could I handle her in a manner of speaking? Finally, about an hour late she walked into the conference room, two Chihuahuas clutched to her breasts, the very model of a beautiful, sexy star. She couldn't understand all the fuss, even if she was delighted with the publicity. She pointed out to everyone that she was Catholic, there was nothing in the show in any sense immoral and she didn't understand why it would be cancelled when no-one had even seen it. She was right too.

But I did my interview and the imagery still stays with me. She was a nice, gentle woman who blew out of the water any idea that she posed a moral threat to the people of Kerry. Newsbeat got great mileage from the story, the newspapers had a ball and I have no doubt that those who opposed the show felt right eejits as time moved on. Sadly though she died in a car accident a couple of months later. Her people denied she was decapitated but said that she had died of head trauma.

I was Newsbeat's junior on the show. Cathal O'Shannon was Newsbeat's main man on the road. I used to envy Cathal and his big stories and his Great Southern Hotel lifestyle on the road while Joe and I were running all over the country doing our three stories a week. But I learned greatly from Cathal who was a terrific colleague and one of the great Irish journalists.

Originally with the Irish Times, he then became one of the top presenters on BBC's Tonight television programme before returning to Dublin to work on Newsbeat. Was he wasted on that show? Some would say yes, I'd say no because he advanced the quality of coverage of provincial Ireland immeasurably but I suspect he was coasting a little. If one was to take today's schedules he would be on a much higher octane programme. However, he enjoyed himself and loved life. He might only have done just one major story a week but he did it with great skill and I was full of admiration for him.

Cathal was a great character, a great story teller, a fund of gossip and information. I lost contact with him for a long time after Newsbeat but we re-established contact through a mutual friend called Liam Kelly who worked in the Daily Mirror and was transferred to Cork to develop their south of Ireland coverage. I got friendly with Liam in Cork and he gave me good leads on stories that he thought would make good television. We have remained friends ever since and meet regularly for lunch. Over one such lunch we came up with the idea of a monthly O'Shannon lunch which he organised.

We invited only people we liked and who had a good sense of fun and the lunches were a huge success over a number of years. O'Shannon of course dominated with all kinds of stories and experiences. I remember one in particular – a television interview which was understandably cut. He was talking to an elderly lady who was something of a socialite in her day, had a great life but was ill in bed for sometime. "Have you always been bed ridden" asked O'Shannon. "Oh not at all I've done it in cars a couple of times as well," she replied.

Cathal's Newsbeat days were followed by a career in PR but he returned to television to make some wonderful contributions including Even the Olives are Bleeding on the Spanish Civil War.

On Newsbeat I was doing sufficiently well for Jack White, then Controller of Programmes, to ring me and ask if I would be interested in joining on a full-time basis. He offered me a one-year contract. I had never met him but he was famous for 'Strumpet City' and so well respected within RTÉ. For him to come calling was hugely exciting and I said I'd go for it, even if it was only a one-year contract.

First though, I had to clear the concept of leave of absence for one year with the Examiner. I decided I would go and see the Managing Director George Crosbie or Mr George as he was known. Back in the 1960s the servial nature of Examiner employees was characterised by the use of Mister or Miss in front of the names of male or female Crosbies. George Crosbie snr was the exception - he was known and addressed as Commander because of his role in the Naval Service during the Emergency.

I explained the situation to George Crosbie, asked for leave of absence for a year and because I had worked hard and loyally for some 10 years I expected to get it. I was surprised and shocked when he said no. But he didn't refuse me on bitter grounds and it wasn't as if they were glad to get rid of me. His reasoning was that no-one who ever got leave of absence returned. George was a decent person and he recognised my shock at his reaction by following up with, "If you want to come back in a year we'll talk about it then". But he made it clear I had to make up my mind about who I wanted to work with.

I loved my time in the Examiner but I wanted to see how good I was. Did I have the ability to make it on television on a full-time basis? Could whatever skill I had translate successfully to a new medium? Could I cope with moving from permanent, pensionable employment to a contract lifestyle?

In spite of my ambitions to be editor, once I got the RTÉ contract offer I never seriously thought about staying with the Examiner; I couldn't reject an offer from RTÉ and live with myself. I suppose looking back over everything when I have had a choice to make I never agonised over it. School versus the Examiner, law versus journalism, newspapers versus television. Each time I knew the winner and went with it. Once the one-year contract was on the table, I was desperate to see how good I could be. I kept telling myself it was a question of trying another medium and seeing if I was more than just a newspaper man. Because, by the time the offer came around, I had a little more confidence in my abilities than when interviewing the Lusitania survivor and being mentally intimidated by the comments of the people in the towns and villages of Ireland.

My poor mother, God rest her soul, was absolutely appalled that I'd give up my permanent and pensionable job in the Examiner. She was very proud of me, both my parents were, of both my work in the Examiner and on television, but she could see no logic in what I was doing. I had the future possibility of being editor and to walk away for a one-year contract was the height of madness in her eyes. But being the good mother she was, having expressed her reservation she didn't try and stop me from taking the RTÉ offer.

Mind you she wouldn't have been able to stop me either.
This was what I wanted and my father understood that. I was
my own man following my own path and I decided to go for
it.

After I took the contract on television I was still living at
home. Most of the guys I hung around with lived with their
families as well because we didn't have the money for our
own place. No one at that time did. The pay cheque wasn't
big enough for a high lifestyle or for me to be getting notions
about myself but I never had a big head. I always saw myself
as a journalist rather than a so-called television personality
and my parents would certainly bring me down to earth if
I lost the run of myself and when you have two sisters and
three brothers, you don't lose your head in that sort of a
house and I never did. Besides, I was never arrogant. In fact
when I was first asked to go on television and didn't think I
would be suited, that was the real me coming through.

****

Out of wardrobe, through the doors, stairs, and the corridor I walked earlier. I head for make-up as I continue to get
ready for this show. The lads on the panel like to leave make
up, which is mandatory, until the last minute but I try to get
it out of the way so I can prepare for the programme and run
through the plans for the night with little interruption. I've
always been that way and I've walked those corridors for an
age getting ready for shows like this one. But it wasn't until
I left Newsbeat that I paced them for the first time and truly
began a career that is still ongoing.

I worked under Frank Hall on the show on a full-time basis
until the middle of '68 and at that stage there was no question of my moving to Dublin as far as I was concerned. I was

a tribal Cork man and I loved my city. On top of that I didn't want to leave at a stage when I thought I could be going back to the Examiner after trying my hand at television. But with those thoughts swirling in my head, I was approached by 7 Days, the groundbreaking current affairs programme run by Muiris Mac Conghail, the editor.

7 Days was a current affairs programme unlike any in the history of RTÉ at that time. It examined forensically the performance of Government and its services and took no prisoners. No RTÉ current affairs programme had done this before and it had a magnificent team of presenters in David Thornley, John O'Donoghue, Ted Nealon, Paddy Gallagher and Brian Cleeve. A galaxy of current affairs stars.

Politics was also top of the 7 Days agenda and Muiris asked me to do a profile of the Cork city constituency on the death of Seán Casey, who was the Lord Mayor and a Labour Party TD. I remember Joe McCarthy saying to me, "This is a test for you Bill for current affairs". "Not at all," I said, "they just know I can do a job like that and I'm based in the area so it's an easy one for them." But it was a test and Joe was right as so often he was. I did the job, researched it carefully, knew the constituency, knew Seán Casey and the bottom line was they were happy with the report which was considered accurate in its projection of what was going to happen in the by-election. After its transmission I was asked to come up to Dublin and was offered a job. I made it very clear that I was interested only on the basis of it being in Cork.

That, I was told by Muiris was not a problem because Cork had an airport and they wanted me for reports from areas like the Middle East, Canada and various parts of Europe. He was quite happy with my base in Cork and I was tremendously excited at the prospects outlined to me. But I knew nothing of the way 7 Days did business. I left Dublin for home and heard nothing more for ages. 'Newsbeat' had gone off the air for summer and I was left there waiting for news but no-one knew anything about anything when I made calls. I presumed the various parts of RTÉ would talk to each other and confer when it came to matters such as staff changes but no. Suddenly in late summer Frank Hall rang and said we were starting again on Newsbeat. He told me that I had better get some projects in the can. It was then I said to him I was going to 7 Days and he was shocked as he had never heard of this. I said it was my understanding that Muiris was to talk to him and in any case I had heard nothing in weeks.

My transfer was finally confirmed at the end of August but Frank assumed I had been negotiating all through the summer. I wasn't because I found it very difficult to get anyone to make a final decision. But he didn't believe me and was very upset and annoyed and felt I was disloyal to the programme. His attitude was brutal with me because he felt very let down and disillusioned. He would have rightly seen me as someone he nurtured, and felt I wasn't honest with him and went behind his back. That wasn't the case.

To say he took it very personally is to put it mildly and from being the guy who gave me my break, he didn't talk to me for five or six years after that until we accidentally met in the Gresham Hotel. I was walking out of the dining room and he put his hand out and said, "Bill O'Herlihy, me and you haven't spoken for a long time but it's about time that we started again". It was a pity to fall out though because I was a big fan of Frank's. We spent a couple of hours chatting and finally he accepted that I was honest but as he put it, extremely naïve.

After Newsbeat, my career was set to go in a new direction and everything about 7 Days was different. It was a traumatic beginning because of the relationship it destroyed between

Frank and I but the worst part of it all was still to come. On September 1, I got a call from Sheamus Smith - he became film censor after Frank Hall, coincidentally, but he had worked for Walt Disney in America at one stage and no-one could pronounce his name until he put the 'h' in it - he was number two on 7 Days and ran all the logistics on the programme as well as being the main producer/director.

"Tell me something, Bill," he said in a voice that told me what was about to follow wouldn't be to my liking. "Are you with us, or are you not with us?" I told him of course I was with them. "Well what are you doing in Cork then?" I told him I was based in Cork. "You are in your arse based in Cork," he said. "You can't be based in Cork and work on this programme, so I'll tell you what you are going to do right now. You are going to go upstairs to your bedroom, you are going to pack a case, you are going to kiss your mum good-bye and you are going to be at a meeting here in RTÉ at 10 o'clock in the morning. And you can tell her that you won't be home." It was that call which introduced me to these corridors.

I was absolutely raging. Not just with the way it had happened and the fact I was being forced out of my natural habitat but also because I'd met my wife-to-be, Hilary Patterson, about six months earlier. She was living in a flat in Cork with a girl who was a friend of my sister's and I first met her outside the Stardust during the day one time, and I met her subsequently at a party. I thought she was fantastic, very attractive, good humoured and lively. At the time I was acting in a voluntary capacity for the Cork Film Festival - this was before I took up public relations as a career - and there was a ball of some sort during the Festival and I invited her as my guest. Surprisingly she said yes and the rest is history.

Hilary is a Dublin girl, a graduate of Cathal Brugha Street

College in institutional management, she joined the ESB as a demonstrator and was transferred to Cork. The primary focus of her job was to provide an expert follow-up service to people who bought equipment from the ESB. She'd be sent to the house of a purchaser to make sure that they knew exactly how to operate equipment. After that, she'd have a cup of coffee, a chat and move on. I thought that was the best job in the world but I was no longer sure that mine fell into that category.

If it had been made clear to me when I first met Muiris that I would have to move to Dublin I would have turned down the job. I wouldn't have given it a second thought and for a while I felt I had been tricked and these people had my life upside down. I didn't have the option of going back to 'Newsbeat' and didn't have any other options either so I said I had better go to Dublin and that was it. The fact Sheamus was right didn't make me feel a whole lot better. You couldn't do that job from a distance. As he pointed out you had to be part of the culture of the programme and I couldn't possibly have reflected that culture if I was based away from the people who were effectively orchestrating it. I might have got away with a year in Cork but then I'd have been told goodbye at that point and I wouldn't have got the chance to do the stories that have enhanced my career and brought me to this point.

It was a big step to go from news features to current affairs and it was a hugely exciting time because the entire landscape was changing. Where previously myself and Joe McCarthy operated very much independently in Cork and made our own decisions. 7 Days was a much more controlled environment. We were on the air twice a week, Tuesday and Friday, and took pride in always being top of the ratings. We had very intense meetings to thrash out the substance of each show and Muiris was very strict in terms of the quality of programming material we delivered. It wasn't unusual for him to say, "I want to talk to you about last week's broadcast". You'd be brought into his office, and he'd continue with, "Look at that question, you missed that, you should have gone much further. There was an opportunity there and you didn't take it. That cannot happen again". So the training focus was fantastic and what I am today is a testament to the influence of Muiris because his was the only training I ever got.

It was necessary too because the standards were infinitely higher. Eoghan Harris had begun the change and revolution in RTÉ's current affairs but Muiris brought it to a new level and was constantly examining government programmes, looking at promises and deliveries. It wasn't that he was negative, but the government had to be called into account for their actions. That was his motto and we lived by that.

He was a far-sighted, tough broadcaster, and he had the intellectual capacity to argue his corner which was important because the government was always complaining about its programme attitude. 7 Days went down like a lead balloon with Government. RTÉ was a new service and government saw it essentially as a propaganda arm. The idea of a forensic examination of government was anathema to the Fianna Fáil administration and over and over again they voiced their displeasure to RTÉ at what they perceived as the unfair treatment they received. There were indeed times when 7 Days was blood sport as David Thornley cut through government spin and got straight to the real substance of the issue.

Of course, everything was not always perfect. I remember at the start of a new schedule Muiris brought us all together and invited also the programme correspondents in London, Bonn and New York. They were there to give us the bigger

Getting ready to face the cameras and take on the world during the opening years of my television career

Me in my younger days and (below) covering the 1972 Olympic Games from Munich with the great Michael O'Hehir

Feeling comfortable as I rose to meet the challenges that were posed by the position of being an RTE anchorman

With my old pals John Giles and Eamon Dunphy and (below) joining
Giles, Niall Quinn and Andy Townsend for the 1998 World Cup

Up against it... the wall in RTE that pays homage to my words *'We'll Leave It There So'* and (below) myself, Eamon and Liam Brady on duty in 2010

Enjoying a night out with Hilary at the 2002 ESB National Media Awards where I was named Sports Journalist of the Year and (below) with the RTE team of John, Liam and Eamon in 2008

Taking time out with Eamonn Dunphy on the RTE set

I simply cannot hide my delight after picking up my IFTA TV Personality of the Year award back in 2007

picture and outline the European and world issues they felt would dominate the year and have implications for Ireland. The meeting was a big success, so much so that Muiris decided to give the programme over to the correspondents and their views on what lay ahead.

So they went on air, live, and were massively authoritative for about 10 minutes. They were really impressive and then, bang, the autocue which carried their scripts broke down. Incoherence replaced authority. No one had a clue where they were in their scripts until the PAs handed in their written scripts many minutes later. Order was restored, the programme limped to a close and the once authoritative presenters staggered from studio.

Muiris was enraged and issued a new edict. No one would again go on a live programme without a copy of the script. What happened that night to the international experts never happened again.

Back then, 7 Days was based upstairs in this very building, where the newsroom now is, and I used to sit directly opposite a person for whom I had huge regard - the economics correspondent John Feeney who was Irish but English-reared and went on to serve in Dr Patrick Hillery's *cabinet* when he was Ireland's Commissioner in Brussels. John, like the others on the show, was working on big economic programmes which required detailed research. Programmes were in the course of being prepared for transmission weeks down the line apart of course from those of immediate news value. But what I liked about 7 Days was that everyone had time to advise, help and support each other. I found it took me some time to find my feet and I came to rely for advice and judgement on Ted Nealon, the programme's parliamentary expert who is a very special person.

Ted was generous and unselfish and red hot on evaluating

situations and identifying stories. He had a great mantra also. I said to him one day, "Ted, you come up with great ideas for stories but you never want to do them yourself and I can't understand that". The rest of us were all desperate to get on air but Ted never seemed bothered and he replied, "Bill, there are only about four or five times in the year when you must be on television and if you are on air on those occasions people think you are on all the time". Face time wasn't for him unless it was seriously important.

I found the show had a completely different environment and it took me time to adapt. I was under the control of producers and editors to an extent I never was in the past and programming was far more serious. It was no longer light and frothy and good humoured, but I survived right through until disaster eventually struck in a way that had ramifications not just for me but for RTÉ current affairs for many years.

I was what Muiris called a field reporter. There were three of us, myself, Rodney Rice and Dennis Mitchell and we were mainly on the road and rarely in studio. Rodney fascinated me, a Northern Presbyterian, Trinity-educated with a real understanding of the Republican agenda who was the programme's Northern specialist. He became an increasingly important member of the team as the Troubles escalated and he had good contacts on all sides. I met Rodney's parents once when we were both working in Belfast and he brought me to his home for lunch. His parents were warm and welcoming but hardline in their views. We had a good time though and afterwards he laughed when I observed, "Rodney, you've certainly outgrown your background." Rodney's work was consistently good, so too Denis Mitchell's who ultimately left RTÉ and went on to become a judge in Hong Kong.

For me, gone were the days of reporting on whether Johnny Murphy reared his goats on the top of Mount Brandon or whether another Tim Hayes wanted to be buried alive to claim 15 minutes of fame. 7 Days was serious stuff and I was working with the best of the best in current affairs. A big change, not easy. But while much has changed, much remains the same. I'm still working with the best of the best only and they've made my job so easy.

CHAPTER 3

On The Road To Nowhere

It's been quiet for too long and as the first half wears on, the attention of the panel wears thin. If Ray Houghton were here, maybe he'd be in the middle of the floor right now showing me his new golf swing and trying to pass on what his coach has taught him in the hope that I can improve my own game. He's a single-figure player and a good teacher but he's doing the co-commentary tonight and the lads prefer other, more cerebral forms of entertainment when they are in studio and the match is struggling and stuttering. With them, it's never as simple as a golf swing.

Finally, during a break in play for an injury, something snaps, the mood changes, and the debate resumes.

"What do you all make of the household charge?" asks Giles.

"A million people haven't paid and I am not going to pay either," says Dunphy so quickly that it's as if he's been waiting for this very topic to crop up.

"I've paid and you'll have to pay at the end of the day unless you want to suffer big cuts in local service," I say, trying to bring logic to matters but I'm wasting my time and that introduction of rationale only makes things worse. "Everyone will have to pay so they are putting off the inevitable."

"No they won't," says Dunphy. "How can they make a million people pay? How can they prosecute that many? It'll never happen. Wishful thinking that, Bill."

"They have to pay," I repeat, "Hasn't there been a suggestion it will, if necessary, be taken directly out of our pay packets?"

"How are they going to get at our salaries," Dunphy again. "Not a hope. You can't do that. I know Fine Gael were a bit right wing in the past, but they can't go that far. Or can they Bill?" he adds, bringing my own links into the conversation.

"They said they can go to the income taxman and get this and that. It's like living in a communist country," says Giles.

He's in his zone now, as is Dunphy. In between them, Brady remains quiet as he takes it all in and avoids getting involved. Liam does, after all, live in Brighton in England. So when they talk politics he is more of a listener and a contributor rather than someone who leads a conversation. Unless it is about football.

Then he is assertive and strong and by no means someone who sits on the fence. His opinions are always carefully weighted and considered, he is not into top of the head stuff and when he has a point of view he presents it powerfully.

Some may see Brady as dour but that's not him at all. He has a very good sense of humour, especially of the absurd and he can be very warm. He is a great member of the panel with a magnificent pedigree as a player and he's experienced also as a manager. What I particularly like about him is that he's quick to recognise a good idea and is totally committed to maintaining the reputation of the panel.

Brady wouldn't be a crowd pleaser like the other two, that's not his nature, but the more I know him the more I like him. He takes a bit of knowing, and while the strength of his opinions and his knowledge of the game comes across on television, his personality sometimes does not. He is always honest, sometimes abrasively so and as an anchor I have felt the cutting edge of his comment when he feels I have to be put in my place. Sometimes as the anchor I don't know what's coming but I enjoy working with him.

I remember well April 8, 2008. On that afternoon Brady was appointed assistant manager to Ireland and introduced to the media in his first press conference. Later that evening Liverpool were taking on Arsenal in the second leg of the Champions League quarter-final and we were on air at seven o'clock. Because of a huge round of interviews, he simply couldn't make our pre-show meeting and we carried on without him. One of the elements we discussed was Arsene Wenger and his antics on the side-line. It was a newsworthy topic which we thought would interest our viewers and we chalked it down for inclusion in that night's programme and thought no more of it.

Brady finally arrived on the set just before we went on air. We emphasised the importance of the night for Arsenal and then showed clips of Wenger showing his anxiety at previous games. He wasn't told in detail about what was coming up, not in the sense the information was held back, it just didn't occur to anyone to tell him. Sky had done something similar a couple of days earlier in the context of Wenger's antics. Dunphy couldn't resist mentioning a likeness between Wenger and Monty Python's Ministry of Silly Walks sketch. Brady went berserk. He really lost it. You could see his face redden but it got worse once the show cut to a break.

Those who know Liam know him as a very genuine guy, but on this particular day he was tired and grumpy. He was in no mind to condone taking the mickey out of his boss and as soon as the cameras went off and the ads came on he stood up and walked right off the set. We all said, "Come on Liam, this wasn't intentional". It was unfair on our part to walk him into it without warning but it wasn't deliberate. That cut no ice with Liam though.

The commercial break was four minutes – could we get Brady back in time? He had left the studio and the floor manager, Tadhg De Brún, went looking for him. No luck. Neither had Eamon. We were back on the air and still no Brady.

The camera focused on me because we didn't want to show an empty seat on the panel before I handed over to George Hamilton at the game.

More discussion with Brady, he accepted there was no conspiracy, no set up and he agreed to return. But it was icy in studio for the rest of the evening. I'd never experienced anything like that in all my time on the show. In the circumstances I walked on eggs when I interviewed him about his new Ireland job and Dunphy did me no favours when he told him, "You jumped the fence baby"! Brady didn't put a tooth in telling us we were out of order and he was deeply resentful about our attitude. He believed we left him down badly. I suppose he was mollified to some extent by our admission that we made a big mistake not to tell him.

Liam resigned his role as Ireland's assistant manager after two years and he was again available to us for Euro 2012. In the early days of the Irish qualification he was very protective of Giovanni Trapattoni. He would not accept what he perceived as populist nonsense suggested by me. He put me down very quickly if I suggested Trap's tactics were out of date and some of his players not good enough and on the night Ireland beat Macedonia in March 2011 he gave me a going over on air. I suggested the Aviva was relatively empty because of the huge disconnect between the Irish team and the Irish soccer public. I said it was because they were playing boring football, which they were and every single one of us knew it. But he pointed out in no uncertain terms that this wasn't boring football, crowds were down because of the recession.

"You are going to say that's down to the football we play," he declared. "That's rubbish. That's down to the working man and the football supporter in Ireland not having any money and that's down to the football supporter keeping that money so he can pay for his heating. Do not go down that road Bill. That is really rubbish. That's below the belt and that's typical of the media here that we have in Ireland. Below the belt."

Everyone watching could see his anger and as he got more emphatic he leaned across and I wondered was I close to getting a punch. But at the same time I was thinking that this is great television and part of me wanted to keep it going for as long as possible.

Brady's view of me is fraught with all kinds of different emotions because he regards me as the guy who hurls the grenade regularly, often with Arsenal involved but primarily with Trapattoni in later days. He is sensitive about these things though less so now. On air he has been constructively critical of Arsenal, which is a change.

Constructive criticism is one thing, but he objects very strongly to populism. He's moderated his attitude to Trapattoni as well recently, the sensitive stage seems to have passed and he can recognise and discuss limitations though he believes the Trapattoni system has served Ireland well and no-one should underestimate the achievement of qualifying for Euro 2012.

****

Studio discussions off-air inevitably fall back on my Fine Gael background and Dunphy loves to rub it in. Sometimes humorously, sometimes very seriously.

My grandfather was a Cumann na nGaedheal TD, became an Alderman of the Cork Corporation and Lord Mayor of Cork as a Fine Gael member. His name was John Horgan and one of my big regrets is that he died before I ever got the chance to sit down and talk politics with him. I was relatively young when he passed on and had no interest in his politics or any politics at that point. But I'd love to have had a long, substantial conversation with him because indeed, from what I learned of him later in my life, he was a fascinating character on a lot of interesting levels.

I know, for instance, he was very hostile to Éamon De Valera because of the Civil War and when he was Lord Mayor would not sit on the same platform as Dev when he visited Cork. That caused quite a stir and it was unheard of at that time. But he blamed De Valera for what had happened and thought that forcing a war was an appalling thing for him to have done to his own people, for his own purposes. It was an act he felt that didn't serve the nation at all and betrayed the people of a new and fledgling country.

Those views were passed on to my mother who was very strongly Fine Gael too, not surprisingly given those genes. My father was a follower of the party as well although in comparison, very passive. With that background I was always a Fine Gael supporter myself but my involvement grew throughout my evolution within 7 Days. But it took a while to get into Irish politics, or more specifically, Irish politics of the Republic of Ireland.

When I signed up for the 7 Days programme they said I'd go abroad regularly but that never happened. In fact one of the few trips I made was to the Middle East and I interviewed the Israeli Prime Minister Golda Meir. What struck me about her was she was very conscious of Irish history and particularly De Valera. She used some Irish illustrations in the course of a very hostile interview I did with her about the treatment of the Arabs.

Niall McCarthy was the producer/director on that trip which included Cyprus and Jordan as well as Israel. We badly wanted an interview with Golda Meir and we began the process of setting it up in Dublin, got confirmation while we were in Jerusalem but we were told it would take close to a week to set up. We went on to Cyprus as part of the trip where I did an interview with Archbishop Makarios, then President of Cyprus. When in Nicosia, though, we got word we could have an interview with Golda Meir the following day so we jumped on a plane and went back to Tel Aviv.

It was a huge press conference - in terms of Jane Mansfield and my experience there, this was Tralee multiplied by one hundred. Golda Meir rarely did interviews at this stage of her career and we didn't know what to expect. It was a major media occasion with journalists from the world's media in attendance - TV, radio and print. It was tightly controlled and carefully structured. Television networks were given their interview opportunities first and in due course it was my turn.

"Ireland, you have 15 minutes," said an official and brought us to where she was seated and I started the interview. After what seemed much less than 15 minutes, the same official returned and put his hand on my shoulder and said, "Ireland, you are finished". I had only got through half the questions though and because I was looking for a substantial feature rather than news interview, I went to the main press conference as well and from the hall I asked questions as part of the writing press corps. But regularly in her replies there as well she would begin with, "As you in Ireland would understand," in terms of the nationalism of the Israelis. She was a very tough woman, impressive in her certainty and in the way she dealt with the media.

I enjoyed the experience immensely and McCarthy was a good director but there was embarrassment on that trip when in Jordan. There, I met but didn't interview King Hussein. He was not prepared to host a press conference and our attempts for a one-on-one interview got us nowhere. But we did get an invitation to a reception which would include media and we decided to go along and get a sense of the king's style. Like the rest of the media we joined a reception line to meet him.

Paddy Barron was our cameraman. I was mic'd up and prepared to meet and chat to the king, however briefly. Finally I reached the King. "Where are you from?" "Ireland", I said "this is my first time in Jordan and I'm fascinated by the current situation". He was very gracious but he made clear an interview was out of the question. Still we had visuals and a sound bite to insert in our story – or so I thought.

When I came back over to our team, Paddy said, "I don't think we got that properly, will you go up again". "I can't go up again," I told him and he said you'll have to. So I jumped in at the end of the line and the king came to the end, looked at me and asked, "Didn't we meet before?" He was a nice man in a very social occasion and he wasn't under any pressure.

It was interesting to work abroad. We were very specific in our objectives, went to specific places, did specific stories and I continued to learn the ropes of journalism. Sadly there weren't too many trips like it. Sheamus Smith and myself went to Emilia Romagna in Italy for a programme on the benefits of joining the Common Market. For all the interviews and research we did, whether we advanced the argument for or against the common market was doubtful. But apart from that I worked mainly in Ireland.

During that era, getting the job done at home was every bit as tough and the characters were as hard as Golda Meir or anyone we encountered on our travels. And although I didn't have all that many dealings with Irish government ministers, I had a couple of rotten experiences that I barely survived. I remember interviewing Erskine Childers who was one of the easiest interviewees because he was a great talker. I was sent to Cork to do an investigative piece on the exploitation of the disadvantaged in Lota. It was a residential school and it was suggested in some quarters that the children were doing a certain amount of work for no money. I investigated it and got the impression there was substance to those claims.

Childers was Minister for Health, and this was a month be-fore a general election date was due to be announced. When Childers came into RTÉ, Brian Farrell collared him straight away, because he was going to be the main anchor come that election and wanted the opinions and thoughts of a key player. Because of this, I never actually met Childers until I was in studio and that didn't bode well given this was a half-hour live programme with nobody but the two of us on air. The first 10 minutes were taken up with my film report from Cork and when it finished I went to Childers, and said, "Minister, as you can see from that, there is clearly exploita-tion of the disadvantaged and I'd like your comments on it".

"Mr O'Herlihy," he said to me, "there is no exploitation of the disadvantaged children in Lota," and he gave a 30-second answer. I asked him another question and he gave me an-other 20-second answer. I asked him a third question and he turned to me and said, "Mr O'Herlihy, this is the third time you have asked me the same question in a different format and I am telling you for the last time there is no exploitation".

I could actually feel the sweat going drop, drop, drop down my armpits. We were about 12 minutes into it and I was wondering how I was going to get through the next 18 minutes. The story was dead and there was nothing left to talk about. This was the nightmare scenario on a live programme. I had to broaden out the conversation but that was playing into the Minister's hands and the programme limped to a close. To this date, that was one of the worst experiences in my broadcasting career.

But *the* worst experience I had in current affairs was with Ian Paisley in the course of the 1969 Northern Ireland General Election. For the first time in nearly a quarter of a century there was an election in the Bannside constituency which for 21 years had returned Terence O'Neill, the Northern Prime Minister, unopposed.

This time he would face Ian Paisley, head of the Free Presbyterian Church. Paisley was one of the great rabble rousing orators and his 'Ulster Says No' message drew big crowds to his rallies all through the constituency of Bannside. The question which preoccupied the media was this: were these big rallies truly representative of the people or were they Paisley rent-a-crowd operations?

I was sent to Bannside to report on the election. From the start I was fascinated by the warmth he showed to RTÉ when told we had a camera crew present at a rally. "We have RTÉ here tonight", he said at one rally, "it is the only station to give me a fair hearing on radio or television and I want you to make sure they get safe passage back to Dublin."

Even by the end of the campaign no-one was certain of Paisley's real strengths but there was a certainty that O'Neill would hold his seat. The question was, by what margin. Finally, it came to the count which took place in the Town

Hall, Ballymena. Paisley, who had a good casual relationship with the media, was in fine form. Good humoured, smiling, joking and chatting prior to the announcement of the result.

O'Neill won but it was effectively a pyrrhic victory – his day was done and Paisley was poised to become the new dominant voice in Northern politics. Paisley knew the significance of the result and reverted to type. The smiling affable figure became the dangerous declamatory bigot as he made his speech from the Town Hall stage after the declaration of the result.

Interviews with Paisley were also done on the stage. I was there for RTÉ and Martin Bell was covering the election for the BBC. We were both going live into our programmes. Bell said to me: "do you mind if I start? My time is tight. I'll give you an elbow in the ribs when I finish so you can take over". Frankly I would not agree to that arrangement today as he got to ask all the obvious questions but, callow youth that I was, I agreed.

After about two minutes it was my turn and I asked my first question. The Town Hall stage was jammed with jostling, celebrating Paisley followers and I was pushed and shoved as I began my interview. Paisley is much taller than me and he stared down at me for a second reflecting on what I thought was a good question when he said, "Young man, can I smell your breath?" Was there ever such a put down on a live current affairs programme? Disaster. I might as well have been mowing the lawn for all the credibility I had. But I stuck to my guns and asked the question again. Even louder came the response, "Young man, can I smell your breath?" "Come on Dr. Paisley," I replied, "I've asked a serious question, what's your answer?" He gave his answer, the interview continued. But, I suspect, no one was listening, I had become the laughing stock of the election.

When we went off air I told him he had done a disgraceful thing to me. "Do you know I am an orange man," I announced, meaning I drank orange juice, not alcohol as at the time I was a pioneer. "No Papist was ever an Orangeman," he snapped back. But afterwards I found out there was a drunk on stage, pushing and shoving and the smell of his whiskey came over the top of me. Paisley presumed the smell of drink came from me and didn't believe me even when I explained I was a non-drinker. At the end as he was leaving the stage he turned and said, "Go easy on the drink now son".

Before his election as a Member of Parliament, Paisley was a dangerous interviewee. He used radio and television for his own purposes and if he was cornered by a tough interviewer there were no limits to his diversionary tactics.

Seán Duignan, one of RTÉ's great news broadcasters, had Paisley in a corner in an interview on RTÉ Radio's News at 1:30 when out of the blue Paisley cut across the interview and said, "Mr Duignan, were you at Mass today?" "No," said Diggy "today is Thursday". "Yes, but do you believe in the Real Presence of Christ in the Eucharist?" "Well, yes." "So why weren't you at Mass today?" That was typical of Paisley's tactics if you were pinning him down. He became a lot more benign when he was elected to Parliament. But in those days for a journalist he was a desperately dangerous subject who many television interviewers carefully avoided.

I never met Paisley again but I was moved on to Belfast also for that election. Gerry Fitt was one of those elected and after the announcement of his result I said to him, "I don't see any point in people like you and John Hume being elected as individuals because I don't think you can achieve anything that way". It was an interesting question given how things developed afterwards. I asked him would he not consider crafting a new party out of the results, which, of course, he and Hume did and the party became the SDLP. I was happy with that element of my election broadcasting but to take that election as a whole, I had been seriously damaged by Paisley. It came as no surprise to hear RTÉ was flooded with phone calls asking why they had sent a boy to do a man's job!

I spent a fair amount of time in the north working for 7 Days and it was a depressing experience to see the imposition of the Bill Craig philosophy of a Protestant state for a Protestant people on the nationalist community. It was awful to see the bullying of people, the discrimination in jobs and housing and the time was ripe for the Civil Rights movement to be born. Little surprise that the IRA followed.

I was very sympathetic to those being intimidated and exploited by the State but it was important to recognise too that there were those who had an agenda that had nothing to do with Republicanism. I had a fascinating trip down the Falls and Shankill with a British Army colonel who gave a very different perspective to the accepted political landscape. "I'll tell you what this is about," he said, as we were driving along the Falls Road. "You see that pub there, he has to pay 400 pounds a week in protection money. You see that shop, that has to pay 200 pounds in protection money. And you see that bookies, that has to pay 100 pounds in protection money."

All the way down the Falls he continued and afterwards we went to the Shankill and he showed me exactly the same situation there. "On both sides it's about people imposing themselves on communities for their own benefit and pretending it's about something completely different. They are all taking advantage of what's happening for financial gain," he said.

Somehow amidst the gloom there were occasional moments of humour. I was in Derry one particular day when there was a disturbance that was a daily feature of life in the city with stones and occasional petrol bombs being thrown at the army. Suddenly the skies opened and the rain came down in torrents and it all stopped. Everyone fled for cover and the colonel on the megaphone lets out a roar at those fighting with them. "Alright chaps, that's it for today, see you all in the morning."

I wouldn't for one minute want to minimise the seriousness of what was happening in Derry in those dark days. But there were times when there was almost a sense of theatre about the disturbances and protests especially if there was television cameras on hand. The availability of television was almost certain to worsen a disturbance of some kind. Many times I saw situations escalate when we arrived with our cameras.

Like the day the army decided they had enough of stones and petrol bombs and had to do something about the situation. The crowd numbered some several hundred and, without warning, the armoured cars drove right into the middle and took out some dozen women and brought them back to where they were positioned. Dismay. Consternation. I watched with incredulity as the rioters formed a deputation and marched up to the army to negotiate the women's release. Taking women instead of men was not part of the scenario but it was effective. Eventually a deal was agreed, the women would be returned if the rioting stopped. It did.

Derry didn't have the level of violence of Belfast and its citizens had much to thank John Hume for. He was a towering figure, dampening down trouble when he could, advocating peace at all times, highlighting injustice through television and radio to the world inside and outside Northern Ireland.

The injustices visited on the nationalist community were

sustained and appalling. The invasion and destruction of houses by the RUC, B Specials and the army were too often indiscriminate and generated the hatreds that fuelled the IRA. The tribal hatreds of those days still exist today.

In terms of spending time in the north back then, thankfully it never got very hairy. Once though, I was lucky. I was staying in downtown Belfast in the Europa Hotel which had the reputation as the most bombed hotel in Europe. One night, myself and the cameraman went to the Theatre Royal to see a James Bond movie and after a half hour the film stopped, the lights came up, followed by an announcement, "Ladies and gentlemen, would you please leave the building."

It was a bomb scare but they were a dime a dozen so there was no great panic. We left the cinema with no great urgency and waited to be called back to see how the film played out. We were standing about 20 yards outside the cinema when there was an explosion and the back of the building went up. In Belfast, anything could happen, any day.

I have one regret from my reporting days in Derry. Myself and cameraman Paddy Barron were filming as we saw a sniper going up to the Walls of Derry. This was after Internment. He was heading for a turret and I said to Paddy, "Come on and we'll go with him". My idea was we'd lie down with him and do an interview but Paddy told me straight out, "You can forget it, I'm not taking a chance like that, I don't want to die." I could understand his point because he would have been much more exposed than me if there was a firefight between the sniper and the army. The army's return fire would have gotten him with his camera a lot quicker than me with a small microphone. So he said 'no thank you' in words more impolite. I was always sorry that we didn't do it because it would have made some great true life television and that's what we were there for.

But as an occasional observer of life in Northern Ireland I felt those who were disadvantaged, both Catholic and Protestant, had a lot more in common with each other than they did with the south or Britain. They were both exploited but the tribal aspect was too deep for them to see that each side was being used by their own and abused by the other side. Indeed, I felt that the northern Catholics and Republicans had little in common with people in the south and were very much a different tribe.

****

Right now, in Studio Four, Dunphy is anything but civil and still abusing me over my Fine Gael links and the household charge. But I am not backing down from this. Not after what I've been through in this field because aside from my time covering the conflict in the north, there were plenty of abrasive characters in the south who make the lads bickering in studio look like a primary school debate.

Neil Blaney is the one I will always remember. He was Minister for Agriculture and Fisheries and was sacked along with Charlie Haughey on suspicion of importing arms for the IRA. Kevin Boland resigned in sympathy. On the day Blaney was sacked by Taoiseach Jack Lynch, I was sent to the back door of the Dáil to seek him out. The feeling was he'd try and leave quietly and I was there to get some reaction if he left through the back door. The instincts in the 7 Days office were correct and he came out the back door. When I saw him coming I asked the cameraman was he ready. He assured me he was, so off I went to doorstep him.

"Mr Blaney, you were expelled from the Fianna Fáil party today, have you anything to say?" He said nothing, so I asked him another question and there was nothing again. So I asked him a third question and which point he took his pipe out of his mouth, turned around, and finally got talking. "Listen son, when I have nothing to say, I have fucking nothing to say." I was delighted with that because that was better and said more about his mood than any evasive answer. But the cameraman didn't get it. I couldn't believe it. I was sick. I met Blaney in Donegal, quite a few years after that. He greeted me and I said to him, "I thought you weren't talking to me?" He said, "I am happy to talk to you now that you are out of current affairs journalism".

What a contrast to leader Jack Lynch. I always found him to be decent and if I had played my cards correctly I might have been press secretary to him and I'll tell you why. I was working in Mayo and got a phone call from Muiris to say Martin Corry - the TD for East Cork - was retiring and a farewell dinner for him was scheduled in Garryvoe. The Taoiseach would be guest of honour and it would be the first time he would be making a public appearance after the sacking of Haughey and Blaney. Muiris ordered me to drop the Mayo story and go to Garryvoe to get an interview – which, let me tell you, was a tall order.

Gerry O'Mahony was Jack Lynch's man in Cork. Known to myself and all journalists as a decent man who would do you a turn if he could. I called him from Mayo, told him I'd been asked to get an interview with the Taoiseach and if he could organise it. He would try, he said, but in the circumstances made clear it would not be a certainty.

Gerry delivered and I went to Garryvoe and set up for the interview. Halfway through the evening, the Taoiseach arrived to us. "Bill," he said, "I shouldn't be doing this. This is a social occasion and I've had a few jars so go easy." "Taoiseach," I replied, "there are certain questions I must put to you but I respect your position." "Fine," he said, "we understand each other."

The interview lasted about 12 minutes and covered all of the salient points and 7 Days were delighted with it. It got a very good reaction when transmitted, all the more so as it was the only considered, sit-down interview the Taoiseach did during the Arms Crisis.

The Arms Crisis was a huge international story and Boland racheted up the temperature when he called the Taoiseach a quisling and demanded his resignation. Following my success in getting the Garryvoe interview, I was despatched to Rathgar to seek another interview. Muiris made clear that because the Taoiseach had been good to us in Garryvoe, I was under no circumstances to doorstep him. If he said no to an interview, I was to accept this and leave.

Which is exactly what happened. You got your interview, the Taoiseach said, you are not getting another today. Fine, I said, we had a few more friendly words and I went back to RTÉ for my breakfast. It was 7:30.

I was at my desk about 9:30am when the phone rang and Eoin Neeson gave me the message 'the Taoiseach wants to talk to you'. He came on the line and said he had more than 200 requests for interviews from news media, both national and international. What would be my recommendation as to what he should do?

Wow. What a dilemma I faced. My duty was to 7 Days but all my instincts were to tell him, don't do any interviews. But I didn't say that and gave him two options. A press conference, which would be suicidal or, if he wanted a controlled response to Boland and the whole crisis, another interview with me. My advice was self-serving, I have to admit, and after further conversation the Taoiseach said he would think about it and come back to me. About one hour later Neeson called to say the Taoiseach had considered everything and decided not to do any interviews.

That was of course the correct decision. I always regretted that I didn't tell him to stay clear of any interviews but my loyalty had to be to the programme in the first instance. But given that he had sought my opinion, I always felt if I'd given him good, objective advice, he might have asked me to join his team.

I was never tempted by the Dáil though, or at least running for a seat. I got a nibble from Lynch's government in the early 1970s and I was asked in a roundabout way by Fianna Fáil to run in Cork but I was living in Dublin at that stage. It wasn't Jack himself, it was someone who said he was representing him, but for me it was never a runner.

I had a very confused attitude to Jack Lynch. I liked him very much as a person. When Cork city was a single constituency I once voted for him and I admired him in a fiercely tribal way as a Corkman who almost transcended politics. I could easily have worked professionally for him but running for a Dáil seat for Fianna Fáil – no way.

My whole background would have rebelled against it but I also took the view that if I decided to run for a Cork constituency while living in Dublin I would have got more Christmas cards than votes. Liam Ó Murchú, television personality, nationally known, is an enduring example for anyone who thinks he or she can represent Cork while living in Dublin.

He ran for Fianna Fáil in the north city in the February 1982 election, while based in Dublin and got a derisory vote. He lost his deposit. Anyone who understands Cork would know if you don't live there you can shag off in the eyes of the people and that was on my mind when I was approached too.

The other nibble I got, in fact it was more than that, was from Joan Fitzgerald, the wife of Garret. She asked me would

I run for President and said I was the only Fine Gael person she believed would defeat Brian Lenihan, who of course was beaten by Mary Robinson. Fine Gael had no viable, interested candidate in that 1990 election and Joan came to me on the basis that she felt nobody else in the party would have been good enough to win. In fact Austin Currie ran and did badly. What authority Joan had to ask me was another matter, but I said, "Look, I'm very flattered to be asked, but there's no way in the wide world I'd be elected". For that reason I never actively pursued it but perhaps surprisingly, in all the years I worked for Fine Gael while on television, no-one ever suggested me again as a candidate for any office and that was the only time my name ever came up.

It was never part of my thinking that I'd run for office. I had my own career worked out and said to myself I'd prefer to be on television and prefer to be in business and my life was very fulfilled. I didn't think running for the Dáil would add substantially to my life. Also, I'm a private person who is not into networking so the notion of having to go to funerals and chicken dinners would appall me. I'd prefer to be in the background and that's the way I have kept it for the most part.

Others from that 7 Days team didn't take that view though and when David Thornley announced he was to run for the Dáil I got a fascinating insight into the political landscape and how it impacted on who got the top jobs regardless of talent. Myself and Ted Nealon were members of Elm Park Golf Club, just across the road from RTÉ and we went there for lunch one day with Thornley and he told us, privately, he had decided to run for the Labour Party in the next election, just months down the line. His ambition, one he felt he would achieve, was to be Minister for Education. Unquestionably he'd have been brilliant at that but Ted told him he hadn't a ghost of a chance. Thornley was shocked.

"Look around you at the heavyweights running in Dublin," said Ted. "You have Frank Cluskey, Michael O'Leary, Barry Desmond, Conor Cruise O'Brien. You have no chance because you are geographically in the wrong place. You will not be a Minister and I am so sure of this I will make a bet with you. I have no intention of running in the next election, but I think at some stage I will go for the Dáil and if I do I will be a Minister before you."

Thornley couldn't believe what he was hearing because he would have seen himself to be on a much higher intellectual level than Ted or any of those mentioned. "If I go in a constituency of my choice it'll be in Sligo," continued Ted, "and that will give me a geographic spread that you simply don't have." And he was right. David ran in Dublin North at the time, was elected in 1969 but lost his seat in 1977 without reaching the heights he had planned or ever becoming a Minister.

But while Ted was right about running in Connacht and becoming a Minister, initially he was forced to run in Dublin Clontarf in 1977 for Fine Gael and I had one of the worst experiences of my life in the course of the campaign. I did a lot of canvassing for Ted despite my television involvement, which of course you wouldn't be allowed to do now. But Ted got all his mates involved, and we canvassed all over for him. On the day of the poll I was sent to the Hill of Howth. I parked my car, had my literature under my arm, went down towards the polling booth and there was a prospective TD called Michael Joe Cosgrave who approached me. He was a Fine Gael candidate as well and this was his greeting, "What the fuck are you doing here?"

"I'm here because I'm helping the cause," I told him, a little taken aback.

"If you think you can come down here with your television background and canvas for Ted Nealon, you've another thing coming," he said.

"But I've been sent here by headquarters," I responded.

"You can fuck off now, you are not canvassing here because you clearly are a Nealon man and you'll be looking only for votes for him."

"I've been sent here and am not moving," I told him.

"We'll see about that," he warned.

With that, he headed off. About 15 minutes later a car came and drove straight at me before stopping suddenly only feet away. There was no intention of hitting me but it served as a warning and four guys got out and two stood either side of me. Wherever I moved, they moved with me. If I went 100 yards, they moved and kept on either side of me. Eventually some Fianna Fáil canvassers who were watching this with a sense of disbelief came up to me and asked what in the name of God was going on. I told them the attitude was that Nealon had been imposed on the constituency and Cosgrave had done years and years of work as a councillor and he wasn't going to be taken out by him. In fact, he wasn't and Cosgrave was elected but he didn't know that then.

Fianna Fáil told me I should be careful but they'd keep an eye on me – ironic that they should look after a person helping their rivals. But they did look out for me and every so often they'd come over and ask was everything okay. I think the polling booth closed about nine o'clock and about a half an hour before it closed, they came along and said, "Bill, if I were you I'd leave now, when the polling booth closes you never know what might happen, so go". There was no violence, simply intimidation on a massive scale and my Fianna Fáil friends, nice guys all, said they'd never seen anything like it in their lives.

Neither had I and I reported Cosgrave to Fine Gael Head-quarters. They were shocked at the level of intimidation, way beyond anything they had seen in a multi-seat constituency. Cosgrave wasn't going to allow Nealon to take what he saw as his seat, he indicated that he didn't want someone imposed by headquarters and his response was based on this. I was taken aback but those who know their politics will tell you that the dirty tricks and battles between candidates of the same party in a multi-seat constituency are greater than any between candidates of opposing parties.

Here in Studio Four the political battle rages. I will defer to the panel when it comes to soccer comment but this is different. And despite my own obvious affiliations I'm quick to remind the lads they have their own affiliations as well. Giles, for example, would be a great pal of Labour TD Aodhán Ó Ríordáin who used to be a teacher before getting into politics. And Dunphy has belonged to every and any party at some stage. I even got him involved in Fine Gael when we started out on this show but he couldn't take it at constituency level and became quickly disillusioned.

He made a contribution to a national strategy committee at one stage, and it was a very good contribution. It was in Garret FitzGerald's time and Dunphy was a big fan of his. He would have been very popular with FitzGerald too but when that era ended, Dunphy switched off and he's moved around ideologically since then although he's very much an independent. I told him he should have run in the last election but he said it was too late, which it wasn't. In my mind he would have walked in if he picked the right constituency but, realistically, it wouldn't have suited him at all. He values his time and if elected a TD, I suspect he might do a George Lee. He likes his pleasant lifestyle too much.

They're going on endlessly about the water charge. Frankly,

I'm bored. "You are out of touch, Bill," says Dunphy, and Giles is on his side. "Blueshirt Bill, blueshirt," says Brady finally joining in laughing. Giles though wants to make his escape and focus on what we're paid to do. He points at the television and the others follow his lead as they get back to what they are here for and restart watching the game. As the first half draws to a close, so does the first political battle of the evening. Again it goes quiet, but not for too long.

CHAPTER 4

This Is The End?

The end of the first half approaches fast and so does the end of Dunphy's dinner.

"Did you make that curry yourself," Brady asks, as he glances down at a plate that has very nearly been swept clean.

"Nope," says Dunphy. "That's all down to the commissioning editor for drama," he notes, referring to his wife Jane.

"Smells good," adds Brady, "great taste, that woman."

"We got it raw in the take away and baked in at home," laughs Dunphy. But he's cut off by a roar from the man beside him.

"Go on my son," shouts Brady. His accent has a stream of English running right through it from years spent across the water and it echoes around the studio as a chance flashes just over the bar. I take out my pen again and make note of the effort for later reference, while Giles tells the floor manager to add that clip to the highlights reel that we'll talk through during the interval.

"They are all over the place," Giles tells me. "There is a goal coming soon. There's no balance in that team, it's just not right at the minute and you'd have to question the manager's selection. There's only going to be one winner. It's obvious."

The others agree. They almost always agree.

Despite the reputation for forceful debate on the air, and the rows that occasionally take place off it, overall we have a very happy programme. Any disagreements over the years about football or otherwise have mostly been forgotten. Thankfully for one and all, bickering rarely continues on into the next day and bitterness is not maintained or sustained. None of the lads would hold a grudge without good reason; indeed the instances of any protracted fights between any of panel, or myself for that matter, have been extremely rare. Given the high-pressure environment, that's quite an achievement and I'd like to think it'll remain that way too.

Brady and Dunphy were anything but friendly in the old days. It was because of the fact that Brady went to Italy to join Juventus in 1980. Dunphy had his newspaper column and there he maintained that the transfer was all about the pursuit of riches. He was adamant that it was the wrong thing to do and he wrote very stridently about Brady. It wasn't out of a dislike for him though. Dunphy was in fact a big fan of his and was sure, in his mind, that the move wasn't doing him any good in football terms. London could have benefited his career, Turin merely lined his pockets, in Dunphy's view.

That was one of the few rows that continued and when Brady joined the panel he dredged it up. They were slightly uncomfortable for a while. I can recall one time, in a discussion off air about tactics and Brady turned to Dunphy and said, "You say that and I will blow you out of the water when the camera comes back on." He didn't say it either because Brady would be intimidating and uncompromising. He is very certain of his own views and strong and convincing in putting them across. Go against him on an issue he's sure of and he will take you apart. He wouldn't feel guilty doing it either.

Yet of the three analysts, it's those two who occasionally go for drinks or a Chinese together once we wrap up proceedings. They are great friends these days and as thick as thieves. The past is very much the past. It's been forgotten. Brady stays in the Herbert Park when he's over here - perhaps it's a sign of the times because it would have been the Shelbourne Hotel a few years back. And maybe it's a sign of our ages that we don't socialise much. It's not because of any hostility towards each other, but the reality is Dunphy lives in Rathmines, Giles lives in Birmingham and Brady lives in Brighton. They all come from disparate areas and it's hectic once they get together. On top of that, the games we cover can drag on, not that far from midnight on occasion.

When Ireland played at home in the past, we used to go to the Berkeley Court after matches. There, we'd chat to all kinds of people and to each other until late before going our separate ways. But, by and large, those days are gone. Now, once the show draws to a close, I go home because there is a lot of work to be done to prepare for a programme. Between that and a day in my public relations business, I'm exhausted. As well, after the last few international matches, we do a webcast. We start at seven, are off the air about 10.30pm and then are on the internet until 11pm at the earliest. So it's obvious why we don't go out so much together.

More recently, at the end of a major tournament, the head of sport would throw a dinner to thank the people central to the show - although that may not be happening any more given the current recession and the financial situation in RTÉ. But in the past it was done as a thank you because the viewing figures have always been huge and, as a consequence, so was the advertising revenue. Not that it's always passed on! It was at one of those post-tournament dinners that Brady was typically blunt. He turned and asked how much

I earned. I refused to say so he took another drink, said he'd tell me what he gets and we agreed. When I said the figure, he couldn't believe how little I got for this show and for doing my best to make the panel look good. You should work in the UK, he said – as if they would understand my Cork accent!

I don't know what each member of the panel is paid but they work hard and deserve every cent that comes their way. Brady nearly always has a six-in-the morning flight after a game. And Dunphy, because of so many other commitments these days, has to put the sociability factor on hold unless there is a special occasion. Since Lansdowne Road reopened we haven't gone out at all but even if we did, Giles oddly would be the one who wouldn't get involved in the outings. He has his own mates, and even though he has a house in Clontarf he usually stays with an old friend Jimmy Sheils who has a place in Rathgar.

They lodged together as trainees with Manchester United. Jimmy, who is originally from Derry, signed for United in 1956 but his career was ended three years later during a training match when he collided with goalkeeper Gordon Clayton. He tore ligaments and severely damaged cartilage in his left leg and was injured for about two years. But Giles kept in touch - a measure of the man - and now, even if Sheils is back in his home place up north, he has a key to the house in Rathgar and will often go straight there after a show.

It's not like we are doing one match a week and heading off to enjoy the rest of our week and laze about either. Everyone else has something to do in terms of a day job. We aren't thinking 'the camera is off, great, let's head for Krystle'. And even if that sort of an idea did crop up, I'd be firm in saying no because that's not my idea of a night out. Personally speaking, I am usually on the prime time programmes which means I'm not off the air until about 11 o'clock either and it could be later still. By the look of this game tonight, despite that chance flashing over the bar, it could be one of those occasions because there's been little other action around the goalmouth.

Am I a social bore? Possibly. I didn't drink until I got married, mind you. I was a Pioneer and broke my pledge by mistake. On my honeymoon in Tenerife, Hilary used to drink vodka and lemon and I drank bitter lemon around that time. It wasn't a wish, but I always said if I broke my pledge, I wouldn't bother restarting it and that would be that. When I took her drink by mistake, I knew straight away because of the taste and just said "Ah shite". But I also said, "Okay, I'll finish it now."

I got into sangria on that trip and ever since, I've enjoyed wine. I'm not a very heavy drinker, though, I never liked pints because I was 31 when I got married and never got into the pint drinking habit. I never frequented pubs to any great extent either because I wasn't interested spending my time listening to people talking crap as I was drinking my bitter lemon. That would have been unusual at the time because in journalism, when I was young, drinking was commonplace and a lot of colleagues would have gone for long, liquid lunches.

If I was to look back on all my years, work impacted on my social life. I started work when I was 16, worked on shifts, some pretty late, had to walk home at night because I'd no car and buses weren't running and I was afraid I'd be mugged half the time. Because I was working on sport at the weekends, I never really got into the pub scene. I went dancing to Cork Golf Club and Cork Con regularly but it was nothing wild, more solid middle class from the very first dance and maybe that sums it up best.

Nearly 60 years ago, when I was a callow youth, The Oratory in Cork was a great place to learn to dance and was jammed every weekend. My first time there I was astonished by the idea of guys on one side of the room and girls on the other. I had no concept of what a dance was going to be like but this was run by nuns, very well monitored which meant you couldn't dance too close. You can imagine the reaction when halfway through the night the music stopped, we were told to kneel down and say the Rosary. Three Hail Marys for purity and then we started dancing again. That was the only time I was ever there but people took it in their stride and that was my introduction to my social life. It left a lasting impression.

I can't imagine that's the case with the lads though. For example if Dunphy sees a piano he'll sing because he loves to and he just loves the attention. He is just so passionate, often contradictory – something which he sometimes but not always recognises. He has what I think is a most essential quality. He can give a dimension to a game others cannot and talk about areas and aspects of a game no-one else would even think of. Frequently he is polemical, political, cultural but always engaging and that is why the audience loves him.

Eamon is a very decent guy and has been friendly to me since day one. He has a good sense of humour and is very self-deprecating. He doesn't take too kindly to other people knocking him but is the first person to knock himself. He has a great sense of fun too. I was with him in Cork recently at a fundraiser organised for Glen Rovers and I was watching Dunphy and thinking how sociable he is. And his sociability is infectious. He loves sportspeople in particular and he was in his element with Jimmy Barry-Murphy, Brian Cody, Donál Lenihan and David Wallace. He has a great capacity to relate to people at all levels, one of his great strengths.

If you are out with Dunphy, he is huge. Everyone wants to meet him, talk to him and he'll have a word with them all, remaining good humoured all the while. When he loses the good humour, he can be tough, bitter, even vicious. But that's the rare side of the man.

Tonight though there'll be none of us stirring and heading for a pub. There won't be a Chinese with Brady either as Dunphy takes one final shovel of curry and pronounces himself stuffed.

"Smelled good," reiterates Brady.

"Course it would, when you spend your time eating that cafeteria food," comes the smart reply. "Anything would smell good after that rubbish."

****

Earlier today, I passed newsreader Bryan Dobson in the RTÉ television production building. I was heading for make-up, and we talked briefly — him about the match tonight, me about the news. I wondered did he realise how close I came to working in his area of expertise long before his time. And I wonder now do the panel realise how close I was to never working in sport long before they joined the panel. A programme I presented did terminal damage to my current affairs career and led ultimately to the downfall of 7 Days in 1971. The options open to me after that meant I was fortunate to move into sport in RTÉ.

Back then I was a field reporter doing a decent job in current affairs, nothing more. The stars were the studio presenters who were rarely interested in going on the road. It was a hugely exciting time in RTÉ. 7 Days was top of the ratings, ahead of 'The Late, Late Show', ahead of all programmes. It was tough, forensic in its evaluation of Government policies and performance, unlike any previous RTÉ current affairs programme so it was different, exciting and unmissable. The public loved it but the Government did not and it came to the boil as a consequence of a programme I did on illegal moneylending in Dublin.

It is important to recognise this: the moneylending programme may have been groundbreaking in its use of hidden cameras and hidden microphones but it was merely a pawn in the Government's determination to put manners on RTÉ's current affairs. I was the one who got it in the neck but the real catalyst was 7 Days' approach to a Government decision to put a referendum to the people on the straight vote against the prevailing multi-seat constituency Dáil structure. 7 Days did a programme on what change would mean to the Irish voter.

The Fianna Fáil Government, under Jack Lynch, believed the multi-seat constituency saddled Ireland with a provincial Dáil where people were more concerned about potholes, heating bills, and septic tanks than national issues. They decided that they'd try and bring in a first-past-the-post system and called a referendum on an issue I believe was absolutely right for the country and would have served us so much better.

One of the big contributors to 7 Days at the time was Basil Chubb, Professor of Political Science in Trinity College Dublin and he, along with David Thornley, presented a scientific survey on the consequence of a straight vote in the next general election. At that stage there were 144 seats in the Dáil and the survey showed Fianna Fáil would have something around 109 if first past the post was passed. No matter the benefit the system would have for Ireland in the longer term, the people were not prepared to give that kind of power to Fianna Fáil – or indeed any other party – under any circumstances. No matter that things might stabilise in the future, the survey had a seismic impact.

A programme perceived as influencing the voters so dramatically enraged Lynch and his Government. The programme saw itself as being informative and giving people full researched background on the implications of the referendum but it was the straw that broke the camel's back. A television station the Government thought should do their bidding had cost them a referendum. After that, they were determined to rein in current affairs.

The 7 Days programme on the first-past-the-post-system was a factual and a careful response to what the referendum would legitimise. But that didn't cut ice with the government. In their eyes, 7 Days was becoming more and more influential and moving further and further away from what they thought RTÉ's purpose was - to support and promote the Government of the day. They decided to put a stop to it and they would take whatever chance presented itself. As it turned out, that would be at my expense.

My programme on illegal moneylending in Dublin became the catalyst.

Illegal moneylending was a massive problem in Dublin at the time. If you had no access to the kind of money you required you went to a lender who gave you money but took your social welfare book and your children's allowance book as collateral. The person who borrowed would go with the lender to the post office, were given the book briefly and collect what was due from Government. Then they would hand over the money and the books to the moneylender and that would represent one repayment. In would cost them a fortune in the end - way more than they ever borrowed and way more than any bank loan - but they had no other choice because they had no other source of money and there were bills they simply couldn't afford to pay.

We did exhaustive research under the direction of Janet Moody and myself with the Gardaí and all agencies dealing with the disadvantaged. The message was overwhelming: this was a hugely pressing issue and a very corrosive influence on people at a certain level within the city. But no-one was willing to talk to us on a tough investigative programme, certainly not face to face. We had to do something that brought home the scale of the problem and in the process dramatised it as well. 7 Days were lucky to have a great cameraman in Paddy Barron and we decided we would use hidden cameras and hidden microphones.

I'd love to say we were at the cutting edge of new technology but our hidden camera technique was as antiquated as a hole cut in a van with the camera sticking out but at the time it was radical and had never been done before. We worked quietly and in secret and filmed the various handovers of money and welfare books in various parts of Dublin. We spoke to a certain number of people, anonymously with their faces blacked out. The irony, given what would follow, was that after myself and the director Joe McCormack came back to RTÉ and edited the programme, Muiris looked at what we had produced and said it was not strong enough. "You haven't got any money lender to talk to you on camera about what's going on," he noted.

We had consciously stayed away from that element of the story but he insisted it needed a money lender to talk about the consequences of someone not paying up. We took to the streets, made our contacts and ended with a moneylender by the name of Golly Greene – who subsequently had a horse named after him. He was quite matter-of-fact in saying 'if you didn't pay you could have your legs broken'. Was he overstating things? Maybe, but I suspect with certain lenders he was calling it as it was. That segment was added and the programme went out on air.

It's hard to imagine now the storm it created and the news and feature coverage which followed the programme. It led to Dáil questions and Dáil debates because there was at once a sense of shock at the scale of the problem and a sense of disbelief that nothing was being done about it. The groundbreaking nature of the coverage by a programme of the stature of 7 Days underlined the appalling nature of the problem.

The modern equivalent would be the 'Primetime Investigates: Mission to Prey' programme with one key difference: that was not authentic; our programme was.

The reaction was so enormous there were calls for an investigation into the problem. The Government agreed but made the extraordinary decision to establish a tribunal of investigation into the programme not the problem. Current affairs was being lined up in their sights.

7 Days had no problem with an investigation. Our research was comprehensive and reliable and the team's political correspondent Ted Nealon told Dáil deputies we had no fear of a tribunal because our research would stand up, there were no loose ends and no overstatement of the situation.

The decision to appoint a tribunal caused a feeding frenzy in the media. Who would chair it? What would be its terms of reference? It wasn't plain sailing for the Government. They wanted three Supreme Court Judges to form the Tribunal Panel – those they approached said no. In the end, three High Court Judges were appointed – Justice Butler as Chair, a former Director of Elections for Fianna Fáil in Dun Laoghaire, Rathdown; Justice Flynn, President of the District Court and Justice Pringle, newly appointed after Bloody Sunday in Northern Ireland.

I learned a lot about the reality of power during the 52 days the Tribunal sat. Once the power of the State moved into action many of those who had given us the most important information either backed off in their support or moderated their views significantly. So many, including the Gardaí, who were central to the substance of the programme did not deliver along the lines of our research. On top of that there was a real danger that myself and Director Joe McCormack would go to jail for not revealing sources.

Even more important than our disappointment with some people we relied on was the decision of the judges within a matter of four days to change the interpretation of the Tribunal's terms of reference. And it was abundantly clear we had to lose, given the way they reinterpreted those terms. They were laid out as the following: "That the allegation of the use of strong-arm methods by unlicensed moneylenders was unfounded. That the numbers and scale of illegal moneylenders operating in the country were far less than those suggested by the programme. That the statements made in the programme purporting to be confessions by moneylenders as to strong-arm debt recovery tactics were entirely valueless."

We had another major problem. We had met many dozens of people in debt to illegal moneylenders who were prepared to give evidence provided they were not named and evidence would be taken in confidence. This was initially agreed, then the Tribunal ruled that evidence offered in confidence would not have the same weight as that in open court and then it was decided that confidentiality was not an option. Those prepared to give evidence backed off because they were too fearful of the consequences – something completely ignored by the Tribunal. It left a huge hole in the 7 Days case.

For 7 Days judgement had been made. Now it was no longer what might be determined but the scale of the damning judgement the Tribunal would make. I can't say we were so surprised. No matter how it might be rationalised, then or now, the Tribunal was set up to screw 7 Days and current affairs generally. Anyone who says otherwise is either a knave or a fool.

It was for this reason 7 Days insisted on its own team of lawyers separate from RTÉ. Former Taoiseach John A Costello and Ernest Wood were our senior counsel supported by Garret Cooney and Enda Marren, who was a tower of strength to me and remains to this day a special friend. It was for this reason too that on the day the tribunal issued a new interpretation of its terms of reference that Ernest Wood stood before them and declared: "This is not a Tribunal, this is a witch hunt."

It was for this reason too that Anthony Hederman SC later to become Attorney General and a judge of the Supreme Court said to me "this is the Alice in Wonderland Tribunal." And he was not talking about the programme! Even this early the question which occupied the legal team was how it could contain the damage.

Appearing before the Tribunal was a gruelling experience with a merciless attack from the State and the counsel representing a variety of interests including, of course, moneylenders. I was five and a half days giving evidence on my script, word-by-word.

One particular passage has stuck with me after all the years. It was after lunch break on day three of my evidence when Justice Butler opened his dictionary and asked of me: "Mr O'Herlihy, would you please define the word classic." I had used the expression 'classic example' and I asked Butler: "You mean in the context of the script, my Lord?" "No, I do not," said Butler, "I want the precise meaning of the word." I argued that since they were examining my script word by

WE'LL LEAVE IT THERE SO: THE BILL O'HERLIHY STORY

word the meaning should have the script context. This was rejected out of hand. I can't remember what I said but I will never forget what Butler said.

"Classic, Mr O'Herlihy," he said, reading aloud from his dictionary, "is the supreme example of the ordinary and I do not understand how a reporter of your experience on a programme of the stature of 7 Days does not know the precise meaning of every word he uses". That's actually in the report that the programme was not authentic and we were irresponsible in the use of facts. That is complete nonsense in my judgment. I'd fight my corner every single time on that because our use of facts was correct according to our research and we were anything but irresponsible.

We did make one huge mistake on the programme however and there is no point in saying otherwise. It was an artistic call made by director Joe McCormack which I did not agree with and protested about before it was used. For obvious reasons scenes were shot at a distance. But to break up the long shots and give some pace as he saw it to the visuals he decided we should have some close ups of books and hands. I told him there was no need for this but he insisted. So we filmed clips of books and hands in RTÉ and they did immense damage. This was revealed in the course of the Tribunal and the headline in the Evening Press was, 'Moneylending shot in Montrose'. That was rubbish because it was just one shot but it damaged the authenticity of the entire episode and gave people with an agenda quite a bit of dirt to throw at us.

The Tribunal concluded that the programme content had been exaggerated too, although claims that participants had been bribed with alcohol to respond to questions in a certain way were found to be untrue. It was a farce and a travesty and comments critical of the manner of the tribunal's establishment were made in the Dáil by Barry Desmond and Garret

FitzGerald. Everyone knew well that the Government had been out to control RTÉ and would do so by any means. In my view and that of others, we had been set up and hung out to dry. It was as infuriating and frustrating as it was worrying.

Years later, I was in the Cashel Palace Hotel and, by accident, I met a relative of Judge Pringle. He told me that the judge had not agreed with the verdict and wanted to write a minority report but was discouraged. The Government, using the Tribunal, wanted to control RTÉ and they did. I'd been caught and shot in the crossfire but the real victim was RTÉ Current Affairs which, in my view, went into decline from that point.

The Tribunal Report was immensely damaging to 7 Days, to myself and Muiris Mac Conghail the editor. A finding that said the programme was not authentic and had been irresponsible in its use of facts could not have been worse for my career.

Ted Nealon was always a good friend and when the report came out he rang and invited me to come to Birr for a weekend when a steam festival would be the big attraction. He wanted me to get away from the whole atmosphere of Dublin and to make sure I wasn't immersed in a sort of self-flagellation over something that was never really my fault. I was a trout in a piranha pool and they were after much bigger fish. I went to Birr and spent a lovely weekend with Ted, Jo and his in-laws. It was a welcome but brief respite. Very brief.

Soon the reverberations of the Tribunal were felt in RTÉ. Muiris left 7 Days and moved to Raidío na nGaeltachta as Ceannaire. I remember, before he left, he walked me around the corridors of the television building and told me I was finished in Current Affairs and it was only a matter of time before I was out. He would not be around to protect me any longer, he said.

Director General Tom Hardiman and the RTÉ Authority were immensely supportive of 7 Days during and after the Tribunal. Muiris believed strongly in the authenticity of the programme but he would have been conscious of the fact that in spite of public support there were forces within RTÉ who would be happy to see the back of 7 Days. It was a very difficult time in my career because the Moneylending Tribunal had tarnished me professionally, regardless of the truth of the programme. I was a soft target. Let me give you an example:

I presented a programme on the closing of a flour mill in the Midlands with the consequence of significant job losses. It was tough, well researched and hard hitting. Shortly after its transmission Hardiman received a phone call from a member of the RTÉ Authority to say the programme was not authentic – those words again! – and he wanted a full inquiry into it within RTÉ. Given the Authority's support for 7 Days this was agreed.

Effectively, that inquiry was a mini tribunal. All film shot, every note taken in research, every interview used, not used, edited according to script was sequestered, re-assembled and evaluated. The programme was found to be authentic in every detail – a decision I expected but it was a hairy time for me. I was under serious pressure and had gone from a hero on transmission of the Moneylending Programme to something of a serious embarrassment by the end of the Tribunal. Did my continuing presence damage the status of 7 Days? Some would say yes, though my colleagues were uniformly supportive. But there was a belief that time was running out for 7 Days – and when the end came it was dramatic.

Sheamus Smith was by now the editor doing a fine job in a tough situation. But under consistent pressure he fell ill and was advised, under medical advice, to take time off. Unfortunately it coincided with the week the British Government announced Stormont was to be prorogued. In the context of Northern Ireland it was a huge story in which 7 Days would be central to RTÉ's coverage. Because of 7 Days' independent role in Current Affairs there was a protocol in place on the appointment of the editor. The staff had to be consulted on the appointment – this was agreed and cast in stone.

Colm O'Briain, who went on to be Director of the Arts Council, was Smith's deputy. Because of his editorial strength, production skills, conviction, and his contribution to the culture of the programme he was the obvious choice to become editor in Sheamus' absence. He did not get the job. It went to Michael Johnston, an experienced producer but with a much more limited current affairs background.

Effectively, Johnston, a pleasant and able producer, was imposed on the programme, which infuriated people already upset in the aftermath of the Tribunal. Had there been discussion about his appointment it might have been accepted but there was not a word to anyone on the programme. The protocol was ignored completely.

I was working on a story in Mayo and when I returned to Dublin there was a note on my desk to be at a meeting on Monday morning in connection with Johnston's appointment. News of 7 Days' reaction to the appointment had spread and there was all sorts of talk about work stoppage which led to real concern about how the Stormont story would be covered – if at all.

The 7 Days team felt it important to meet the Director General who had been a very good friend to me and powerful advocate for the programme during the Tribunal times.

He said no. Understandably he would not meet anyone on what was perceived as an unofficial strike. This was not at all the case because all of us were aware of the significance of the Stormont story and wanted to work on it.

Eventually Ted Nealon came up with the formula that we were available to work but professionally unable to do so because of the Johnston appointment. This was acceptable and the meeting was agreed.

The Head of News and Current Affairs, Jim McGuinness, attended the meeting with Tom Hardiman. McGuinness was a strong and effective Head of News but no friend of 7 Days. His evidence to the Moneylending Tribunal was unhelpful in my view but, to be fair, fully in line with the feelings he expressed about the programme. Still, I felt he had let us down and I had no sense that the meeting was going to be an easy one. I was absolutely right – it was an acrimonious, sometimes heated meeting where we made plain 7 Days was not receiving the support it had in the past.

But the climax had yet to be reached. It came when Rodney Rice asked this question of the D.G.:

"There's a lot of talk around the station that 7 Days is coming off the air in the autumn schedule, can you enlighten us?" he asked.

McGuinness stepped in and said in his soft Derry accent, "I'll take that, Rodney," and delivered a bombshell. 7 Days is coming off the air in the autumn schedule, it is being replaced by another current affairs programme, we don't know what the name of it will be, we don't know who will be working on it, but we do know who won't be working on it. Bill O'Herlihy will not be working on it. You will not be working on it. Dennis Mitchell will not be working on it," he said.

There was a stunned silence. Finally Chris Darby, who was one of the best directors on the programme, broke it. "Well I did my best work with Bill O'Herlihy, Rodney Rice and Dennis Mitchell and if they are not good enough for the programme I won't work on it".

Virtually the whole 7 Days team attended the meeting. Brian Farrell was tied up in UCD but said it wasn't his fight anyway and Joe McCormack, who was seeking a staff job, said he would not jeopardise his chances by attending and we were fine with that.

What followed Chris Darby's comment was amazing. One by one, each member of the team said they would not work on the new programme under these conditions. It was an extraordinary demonstration of the loyalty and team spirit of 7 Days which had been honed in the toughest conditions. Hardiman and McGuinness were surprised to put it mildly, their plans for the new season scuppered, at least temporarily.

That staff boycott was not sustainable and we all knew it. But we knew too there was no way they were going to have me back on a high-powered current affairs programme. Dick Hill, with whom I worked on Newsbeat and who went on to become the boss of RTÉ 2, told me subsequently of the strategy behind the decision to axe 7 Days. Sacking me would appear to be vindictive, they felt, so taking the programme off the air was the simplest and cleanest way of taking me out of current affairs without a negative fallout.

So here I was, married only a matter of months to Hilary, facing the prospect of being without a job but with a two-year contract in place and some 20 months to run. What lay ahead, I wondered, if anything? Would I be paid off or would they let me sit around doing nothing for the next 20 months? To my delight I had a number of options. Colm O'Brien, now editor of Tangents, a soft current affairs, news features programme, offered me a presenting role. To my astonishment Jim McGuinness offered me a job in RTÉ News.

McGuinness said he didn't know exactly what I'd be doing

within news but he knew for sure I wouldn't be doing any
social affairs programmes. However, I was advised that I'd
be mad to go into news because I'd end up as number two
behind Tom McSweeney in Cork and that would not be a
step forward!

I also got a nibble from the Irish Times which tempted me.
In fact it more than tempted me. I would have gone, assum-
ing genuine interest. Maybe my television career, which I
envisaged as being in news and current affairs, may have been
over. But I tried to stay positive and thought seriously of going back to newspapers.

With that in my mind, I went along to Oliver Maloney,
then Director of Personnel who subsequently became Director General of RTÉ. Oliver spent considerable time with
us at the Moneylending Tribunal. I got to know him there,
admired him enormously and valued his advice and friendship. He was empathic and told me not to think of leaving because I had done nothing wrong and if I left, people
would assume automatically that I was either fired or had no
alternative in RTÉ. It was great advice. Instead he asked me
what I wanted to do and I told him I'd like to go into sport.
"You'll go there," he said. What a friend, what great advice.

Sport was what I wanted for a couple of reasons. I very
much enjoyed working on radio sport in the past and I felt
too it was important to keep my head down. I knew my current affairs career was finished. I didn't want to go to 'Tangents' which was more along the lines of 'Newsbeat' and I
didn't see any real benefit for me to take that road. Sport was
the way to go.

It took some time though, longer than I anticipated. I
learned later there were long discussions about my going
to sport and for a period of about eight weeks I was doing nothing more than just hanging around. I didn't care

though; I was just married, had a job for close to two years and there was the potential of more if things worked out. I was sure they would too, when, finally, I was told I would be joining sport the following Monday.

My new boss was the legendary Michael O'Hehir. He was not there on the Monday, he was off racing for a couple of days and when he returned I was called into his office to learn more about my new role. "Bill, I don't want you, but you are welcome," were his very first words to me. He told me my hard image was wrong for sport. He was adamant it wouldn't serve me well and it wouldn't serve the sports department well. "I don't want you at all," he continued. "You are here now but I can tell you this for nothing. You will not be broadcasting for a minimum of six months."

Fair enough. It wasn't the welcome I expected but after everything I'd been through, I couldn't have cared less. That may seem odd but, given the battering to my career, I was happy to learn other skills like editing and I really didn't give a damn as long as I had a job. When he told me the score I just accepted it and said that it was fine with me. That was the end of the conversation and I left his office. I came in the next morning; he called me into his office again. I didn't know what to expect after our opening conversation but I was very taken aback with what followed.

Séamus Ó Riain, a lovely man from Tipperary who was the 22nd president of the GAA, had, with Pat Guthrie, started an organisation called Féile na nGael whose objective was the development of juvenile hurling and O'Hehir told me he'd be in Dublin that Friday and wanted to promote it by way of an interview. He told me to do the interview. To say I was surprised would be an understatement. "But you told me yesterday I wouldn't be on air for six months," was my response. "Well, that was yesterday, today I want you to do it," he said. I went and met Ó Riain and my interview was broadcast the following day. Subsequently I worked with Séamus on Féile and he was one of the most unforgettable men I have met.

It got better from there and my relationship with O'Hehir improved. It got to the stage where, looking back, I can now say that he was important in the development of my career and helped me get to nights like this one. On one particular occasion, months after I joined Sport, we were in a meeting and I'd spent a lot of it spouting out ideas for stories. Shortly after it ended he came over to my desk, put his arm around me and he said loudly in front of everyone so they could all hear, "Bill, I know I didn't want you, but thanks be to God you are here." That meant a lot to me.

Some people rang RTÉ and said it was terrible to see Bill O'Herlihy reading the racing results but I was really enjoying myself. I met Jim McGuinness of all people some months later and he said to me, "Well Bill, you and I have had our differences but I have to tell you I think you are doing very well in sport, that's your correct niche." I don't think he was just paying lip service. He was right too. I'm a great believer in the Lord working in mysterious ways. I'm not so sure I'd have lasted this long if I was in Current Affairs. Certainly if I wanted a long term career in television, it was the right way to go – even if it was by accident rather than design.

Everything took off from the time I transferred to Sport. In many ways it was predictable in its output – Gaelic games, racing, rugby and soccer internationals and a couple of magazine programmes from time to time. Sports output was determined by the product available to an Irish broadcaster. Today everything is utterly changed.

I made my contribution to the nightly sports news output and to the magazine programmes but my big break came when I was asked to present the 1972 Olympics with Michael O'Hehir. O'Hehir, as Head of Sport, was the main presenter in week one, then he went to Munich and I took over as the main presenter.

The second week in Munich was the most traumatic in the history of the Olympics when Black September attacked the Israeli Team, assassinated athletes and coaches and took hostages. What began as sport became a major current affairs story and I happened to be the presenter in the right place at the right time. My current affairs training served me well and I demonstrated my skills in co-ordinating the story of an appalling tragedy.

In spite of the tragedy it was decided the Games should continue. This was the right decision because a cancellation would have left future Olympics open to all kinds of terrorist threats.

Munich, though it seems crass to say it, was important to me in terms of career development. I had shown what I could do at a time when profound change was enveloping sports broadcasting and three people, Fred Cogley, Tim O'Connor and Mike Horgan, were changing the landscape forever. We were entering a new era of sport – of greater production of Gaelic Games, coverage of national and international and cross channel soccer, of evaluation and analysis of sport. It was an exciting, dynamic new environment and I was privileged to be part of it.

****

The end of the first half approaches fast and once more the latest stack of soft drinks have been whisked away moments before we go back on air. Dunphy's empty plate is taken too and he's told from the floor his shirt is missing a button around the tummy. Eyes focus in on his midriff. It's the first he's heard of it but he's quick and he's funny and he just sucks in and laughs, before pulling close enough to the desk so it's out of sight of the cameras. The great thing about our programme is its humour on and off air. People see at home the real characteristics and characters of the panel who are allowed to express themselves and be themselves which is very different to some of the coverage you see across the water.

The panel seems to strike the right balance between humour and analysis, laughter and sternness and they have earned a very special place in Irish sport.

Sometimes, depending on the game, I get a little desperate. I'll look at the lads and say we have 25 minutes to fill and nothing more to say. But Giles will always tell me there will be no problem and there never is. It flows because the three analysts are so different, Dunphy something of a soccer and sports philosopher, Giles a brilliant reader of a game, Brady pragmatic and full of insight. Like I said, we are in some respects like a repertory company each of us knowing and playing to our roles.

Dunphy has a great sense of television. About a year ago I was about to ask a question and I lost it live. I said, "Well lads I was about to ask you something and it's gone." "I'm delighted," said Dunphy quick as a flash, "because I've wanted to ask you this question for a long time." By the time he had finished having a go, the question had come back to me. That is another example of what makes him different. Dunphy is the perfect panellist and Giles and Brady the perfect analysts.

Thankfully I don't need Dunphy's speed of thought often though, because that is the only time that I've had a brain freeze.

But if I really lost it, I know the lads on the panel would recognise the problem and take over and because of this comfort that is perhaps one of the reasons I've never really lost it. Those who watch our soccer programme regularly will recognise it's not all about answering my questions. Panel discussions should be exactly that and I tell the lads I don't want them talking to me all the time, I want them to talk among themselves. The guy in the pub or at home would much prefer to see the three of them arguing amongst themselves and that's part of our philosophy. We are comfortable but my role as anchor is clearly defined. I question, I probe but I am not an analyst. I would be put in my place if I thought otherwise and frankly the programme would lose something.

Running a discussion programme on any subject including sport requires one thing above all: the ability to listen, to go with the flow, not follow a set pattern of questions that take little account of the trends of conversation.

In my early days Michael Parkinson was my role model. His great skill was that he listened, took in the answers and he didn't try and dominate. By listening and following up what was said to him rather than coming in with a whole series of set questions, he made people relax, made people interested because he was interested and I learned from him. Gay Byrne had the same gift, a brilliant interviewer and a great listener. I remember a time before the tribunal when Jim McGuinness came into the 7 Days office. "Look at you all, you think you are the great current affairs people but Gay Byrne has achieved more in one programme than you have in a year." He was no lover of our work but he made a very important point because Gay Byrne's 'The Late, Late Show' moulded Ireland in its attitudes and had a seminal influence on what we are today.

But perhaps the biggest influence on how I present programmes has been Paddy Downey who used to write about

Gaelic Games for the Irish Times. I was a great fan of his writing which had a simplicity and clarity while, at the same time, so much penetration. I was talking to him in a press box in Cork when I was a young reporter and our conversation had a seminal influence on my career and on my programming. I said to Paddy, "How do you approach it?" He told me that he had a friend, in Barna in Galway and she loved the game but didn't fully understand it. "I always write with her in mind," he continued. "I think of her reading what I write and enjoying it but also I like to think she will gain knowledge of the game from it." I keep that thought with me and that's how I work in the way I do my interviews. I try and get information across even at my own expense.

Sometimes the lads give me a hard time for asking an obvious question but they, like me, are aware of a survey taken some time ago which indicated fewer than 40% of the audience understood the game. So, sometimes, the obvious question is the one people at home or in the pub are asking as well. That's the distinction between anchor and analyst and they do respect me journalistically.

Their being here is down to the evolution in sport that began when I came into this department and from a tough learning experience. We had to find out about the need for a panel the hard way. Or at least I did. It's difficult to believe when I take a look at my surroundings now, but there was a stage when I was alone in studio covering games. The last time that happened was when I presented a Cup Winners' Cup final played in Switzerland between Dynamo Kiev and Ferencvaros in 1975 watched by a small crowd. A game of very few incidents, no panel and short commercial breaks.

I had to fill 12 minutes by myself on the game at half-time. A nightmare would be an understatement. I paid for it. Dunphy wrote in his column afterwards, "It was quite clear

O'Herlihy has no knowledge whatsoever about soccer and that was one of the worst performances I have seen." We had just started working together at that stage! He was right and I said to RTÉ after that, "I'm not doing this ever again." It only exposed my lack of knowledge and there's no benefit to the viewer with 12 minutes to fill and nothing to say. There was never another European match without a panel so at least it had the effect of ensuring nobody was ever put in my position again. If there had been six goals it would have been no problem but there wasn't even one substantial incident and I still had to fill the 12 minutes.

Dunphy had no problem having a go at me and in his early days he was famously outspoken. The first interview I did with him was when he came back from Chile as a member of the Irish soccer team. He was very much opposed to the Irish team going to Santiago for a friendly because of the Pinochet dictatorship but he went anyway in spite of his strong words. Giles used to slag him and say he was first on the plane. I was doing a programme called 'The Sunday Sports Show' with Tim O'Connor as editor. It was a very good, somewhat radical programme, part satirical, part serious. On this occasion, I did an interview with Dunphy down the line as he was managing the University of London soccer team at the time. He was expecting a soft sports chat but got instead a tough current affairs interview.

He really had to work hard to get out of the hole he was in. "You skewered me," he joked afterwards. But I had to because there was a massive contradiction between his words and his going there. But that started our relationship. He well remembers it and said it gave him a respect for me from the word go. We've worked well together.

We get ready for some half-time chat, Dunphy is due to start the analysis and I look at him and think about how my relationship with him has only been strained once. I had one very serious row with him during the World Cup of 1982 in Spain and it came out of nowhere in the course of a Northern Ireland game.

In studio, Dunphy was a constant. David O'Leary was on the panel too and Dunphy didn't really get on with him. In fact he hated the idea of an analyst who was careful to say nothing in case he might insult someone. As well as that, Jim McLaughlin, who was Dundalk manager but soon after would take over at Shamrock Rovers, was a panellist. McLaughlin had himself played for the north for a spell during the 1960s and was quite prolific in front of goal but on this occasion was giving out stink about Norman Whiteside. Dunphy turned to him off air and said, "You have some cheek talking about Whiteside. You encourage that Dundalk team of yours to be real hatchet men. You're talking about Whiteside, you do the same every game in Oriel Park. So that's bullshit. I'm going to do you over when we come back on air."

I thought Dunphy was wrong and didn't know why he was acting like that. Naturally, I tried to talk sense. "Eamon," I said to him, "what relationship has Dundalk to the World Cup. You are making a fool of yourself. This is the biggest stage and now is not the time or the place so just don't do that. It's cheap." He said nothing so I thought no more of it and we came back on air and I was having a pleasant conversation with McLaughlin. The matter of Dundalk was never raised but Dunphy got very withdrawn as the second half went on.

It came to the end of the match and I often play to Dunphy because he gets a discussion going. I asked him a question and he said, "Yep." I asked him another and he said, "Nope". I asked him a third and he said, "Yep". So I said to camera, "Very obviously you aren't in a talkative mood and he said, "Yep". We continued, the programme finished and I asked him what the hell was wrong with him that he went on like that. "Nobody has ever and can ever call me cheap," he shouted. I tried to explain to him that I wasn't calling him cheap, but I thought the comment about Dundalk was cheap and that was a different thing altogether. "You can fuck off now, I won't put up with that," he said and stormed out of the building.

The next day he wasn't communicating properly either, perhaps a little better but still not good for television purposes. So our editor Tim O'Connor said we'd have to sort it out and we had a long discussion about it. I said to him, "Eamon if you don't talk to me one of us will be gone and it won't be me, I'm the anchor. It doesn't serve either of our purposes, we get on and are friends, and there is no point going on like this." He agreed, probably thinking he had made his point and we shook hands. That was our only row. It went on for about 48 hours and I found that very distressing because I'd huge respect for him and I wouldn't dream of calling him cheap. He got it all wrong.

I've never had a row with John Giles. He has a much more even temperament and would never dream of saying "Yep" and "Nope" even if he did have the hump! John has always been to me something of a mentor and our relationship is very much the master and apprentice. Dunphy's relationship with me is more journalist to journalist. But the lads like working with me. I know they do because I'm committed to making them look good. And tonight there is no 'Yep' and 'Nope' as we close in on the interval.

CHAPTER 5

Perspective In Sorrow

People don't realise the work that goes into this show. It's not just those of us on the air; it's not just those on the floor and in the gallery either. Scattered through this building are those who make this programme happen and contribute substantially in their own skilled way. So, as the lads dissect the first half and talk over the clips they've picked out across the opening 45 minutes, I get thinking of those the audience at home can't and never lay eyes on. They are out of sight of the public but shouldn't be out of our minds.

After I met Bryan Dobson, I went to make-up. It's strange in there and the brilliantly bright lights and the rows of mirrors mean there's no getting away from either age or imperfections. Off with my jacket and the make-up girl Julie began the process of hiding years of work and stress, worry and joy, in just a few brush strokes. We got chatting and she asked me about my children and grandchildren. "They are all great," I said, as she dabbed my face with a sponge and the conversation turned to other matters. "Medicine is so much cheaper in Europe," I told her. "There's a cold spray I use which covers the marks and gets rid of the imperfections left behind after cancer treatment. It's expensive here but half the price there." She agreed about the cost as she looked closer at the marks on my face.

I'm quite shy about those reminders of what I've been through and sometimes it's uncomfortable looking in the mirror straight after treatment. But, worse, there's no getting away from the disease itself either, especially when it comes to my family. It has followed us around like a shadow, always lurking, always merciless.

My father died when he was 75 but it was my mother who first introduced us to cancer and the misery it brings, and has brought, in vast quantities to our family. She was 73 when she passed away from it and that was the end of our parents, of a wonderful upbringing, of Myrtleville and Ballycotton and, in many ways, innocence. Worse still, for Mum and us, it was cancer of the brain — at least it went all the way to her brain — and that made our time together at the end all the more difficult.

I was always very close to her and we had a special relationship. In truth, despite her occasional objections to the paths I took and roads I walked in life, I was spoiled by her, perhaps as my wife Hilary says because I was the eldest of her six children. I can still remember the devastation in finding out she had the disease and the prognosis that she had only months to live. My sister Mary called to tell me and if it was tough on all of us, it was hardest of all on her. She never married and she looked after Mum and Dad in her way — not at the expense of a social life or anything like that, mind you. So it was she who would have taken Mum for tests and was first to learn of the horrific results.

Mum was sick for about six months and spent her dying days in the Bon Secours Hospital in Cork. Hilary and I would drive down to see her and those days were extremely upsetting. It wasn't just because she was dying; it was because of who she had been and what she became. Where once we had a very strong, articulate and intelligent woman and mother, cancer changed her into a person who was very hard to understand. It took away all the positives she brought to the world. Towards the end she lost her speech, then her sight, and finally her life.

I remember her lying there struggling to get across her thoughts. I'll never forget that. She knew what she wanted to tell us but couldn't get the words out and we had to interpret for her and fill in her gestures with our own words. That became very frustrating for her and hard for us to see.

My elder sister Margaret constantly went to Cork in the closing stages and she was the first to recognise that Mum couldn't even say her prayers. Against the backdrop of our upbringing, that was terrible for her because a part of our childhood and teenage years was the Rosary. It was said in our house every night without fail. Even if we were out playing, there was no avoiding it. My father had a very distinctive whistle which you'd hear a mile off. We knew we had to go in as soon as we heard it. We'd resent having to leave a street match but there was no discussion and we'd have to wait it out through the Rosary before the game outside could resume.

As her faculties disintegrated, not being able to pray was so sad because that was so important to her. And as she was dying all of us remembered how she had been such a great mother and great person, full of fun, intelligent, knowing, and protective of us and we were forced to ignore the shell of a person now in front of us.

Mother's cancer was just the start. Years later both my sisters got cancer as well. Mary was the younger of the two but was the first to die. We were great mates and always got on like best friends as well as siblings and she told me this extraordinary story without realising the implications.

She was driving to work one day and rang me shortly afterwards to say the strangest thing had happened. All of a sudden, she said, she couldn't see out of one eye. I was naturally worried and asked her what she did about it. She clearly wasn't as worried as I was and, typical of her, said she just carried on and did her day's work. She was never a woman to overreact or, in this case, merely react. But on her way back that evening it wasn't any better so she finally decided to do something about it. She called into the same Bon Secours where Mum had died, they gave her tests and, shortly after, the bad news that meant she was going to die very soon as well.

She had been in remission for six years but was never released from hospital after the results of the tests became known and she was dead in about three weeks. Amazingly, she took it all in her stride, a measure of the woman and her strength and nature. Somehow, she was positive right until the very end but if that was extraordinarily courageous, it was extremely fitting, too, because throughout her life she was full of personality and vitality.

It's perhaps a strange thing to say, but in one way she was lucky, because there was such a short space of time between that incident in the car and her passing. That, though, was small consolation to us who loved her and we were utterly devastated. Yet when we were at our lowest point, it all happened again and within little over a year, we lost my big sister Margaret. It was an appalling time in our lives as nothing prepares you for the loss of one sister, never mind both.

Margaret was a wonderful sister too. She lived in Athlone and over the years when Mary was sick came down to Cork, looked after her and drove her here, there and everywhere while she was still allowed out. But on one such trip down from the midlands she got pins and needles in her legs and it turned out that something so innocuous was the start of a major cancer. Sadly, she had a long death over the best part of 12 months. She was in and out of hospitals and ended up in a home because she needed constant nursing. That made it even worse than our experience with Mary. Both were wonderful people and sisters, were very special and vital in our family.

Both rarely leave my thoughts, even to this day.

Looking back, I consider Mary to have been the anchor of the family in later years and a focal point for all of us because she lived in the family home. After Mum and Dad died we gravitated there to reminisce and strengthen our bonds, and she held us all together like glue. With the two girls gone though, myself and my three brothers Jack, David and Peter are committed to meeting twice a year and we do. I have loads of phone contact and regular meetings but as a family we make sure that every summer and winter we get together. That's important, even if we come from all over, as my brother Jack lives in Letterkenny, David and Peter live in Cork and I'm a tribal Corkman living in Dublin.

It may seem strange to many, but our sisters' deaths so early in life never stopped us going to Mass. Faith was ingrained in us and still endures. As a result of my belief, when I was ill I would place myself in the hands of Our Lady and I knew full well I'd be looked after. Every day I ask Our Lady to put her arms around Hilary, Jill and Sally and nothing bad has ever happened to them. And even when my sisters died of cancer it wouldn't have ever occurred to me to question God. That's just part of the natural progression of life and while hardship and sorrow might test your faith, it shouldn't destroy it or your belief in infinite truths.

There was a religious theme in my childhood in many ways so it's hardly surprising that we were not permitted to miss church. There was no question of our not going to Sunday Mass. That was how it was until we were about 18 and we could make up our own mind at that stage. But by then it was such a part of my life for so long I was never going to change my ways. It wouldn't occur to me now not to go to Mass and if I didn't go on a Sunday I'd have a huge crisis of conscience. In fact I try and go each day and it's anything but a chore. I quite enjoy it and I'm very lucky that my office is close to St Mary's on Haddington Road. I like the idea of stepping away from the working world for just a little while and commune with God for half an hour each day.

Because I believe in the Lord and the Hereafter, I believe people with faith should display it publicly. That's why I go to church as often as I can and it's why I try to be honourable with people around me and put my beliefs into action, just as my father did many years before me. I could have sold my public relations business, O'Herlihy Communications, and made a lot of money some years ago but I didn't because, at the time, those working for me would not have been guaranteed a job. After the contribution they made to the success of the business, it wouldn't have been right. Funnily enough, none of those I sought to protect are with me today.

I have been blessed by the Lord, blessed with two gorgeous girls, Jill and Sally, a lovely wife, Hilary, and lots of good things have happened to me in my life, in spite of those tragedies I've had in my family. I was in the right place at the right time when it really mattered and I survived a heart attack and cancer and came out the other side, a stronger person for having had those experiences. Say what you like, but I've no doubt there was a Greater Power watching over me and the end result is that not only am I still here, I'm still in this studio broadcasting when others I once worked with have long retired or passed on.

****

People don't realise the quality of the talent on this show. Little has happened in the opening half yet still the lads have so much to say and so many opinions to squeeze in between the ad breaks during the interval. Their conversations explore avenues like no others. They see the bigger picture, are always honest in their assessments, which is why our audiences are consistently big. At times like this I feel as much a timekeeper as an anchor and I wait for our editor Eugene O'Neill, in the gallery, to tell me when to cut them off. I have so often encouraged the panel to discuss games among themselves because it makes for a far better television spectacle and promotes compelling debate. On too many stations it's just questions and answers between anchor and analyst and, quite frankly, sometimes there's nothing more boring. We always seek the right balance.

"That's just played into their hands," announces Brady authoritatively. "Key players didn't show the right kind of composure, that you'd expect of guys at this level. They didn't play beautiful football but they couldn't handle them at crosses and setpieces either."

Taking it further, Dunphy goes to an extreme. "Careers are on the line and they'll have to show a great deal of character from here on in or those careers will be over." It's not exaggeration, in his mind, he has considered the facts, truly believes and he's hugely passionate about his beliefs. For those reasons he always believes he is right.

"Teams coming out for the second half, Bill," comes word from the gallery into my earpiece. "Twenty seconds and then back over to the commentary team." I wrap up their half-time discussion because I must, but reluctantly because sometimes I could listen to them all day when the adrenaline is flowing and the comment is good. When thinking about disease and death, some people might see a soccer show as trivial. But this is one of the good things of my life and I never forget how lucky I am to be here. Some things outside of my control have taken life, but this is in my control and it has added hugely to the enjoyment of my life. Had it not been for television, I don't know what would have become of my life after my heart attack. It wasn't just a job then, but a saving grace, too, and a vehicle to bring me back to normality and convince me things could go as they had before.

I still find the circumstances surrounding my heart attack particularly remarkable. At that stage I was in my early 40s and had never been seriously ill. I felt I could shrug off any-thing and everything that came my way — especially having come through the tribunal and remained in RTÉ. I had no reason to think any other way, and having become settled in sport, I saw myself going through life with few difficulties. It all seemed to come easily and everything was working out for me.

Did I foresee a heart attack? Never, but I recognised the stress associated with television and my growing role in pub-lic relations, both tough industries where results matter.

I got that heart attack just before the 1984 Los Angeles Olympics and on a day when I had a clash of meetings. It was the day of the final meeting of RTÉ's entire Olympic team — the home crew and those heading for California all came together to underline the communication imperatives of the Games' coverage. Tim O'Connor chaired it and dur-ing the discussion, made clear I would anchor the primetime show and said, "Bill O'Herlihy is our star. He is to get every support". Hallelujah! Finally, recognition, I thought. But I didn't realise my priorities were about to change drastically.

The other meeting that day involved one of my public relations clients. It was a company called Parc for whom I worked for many, many years. They were an offshoot of Aer Lingus and had a hospital in Baghdad which was rated the foremost tertiary hospital in the Middle East. I did a lot of promotional work for the hospital which had a constant requirement for nurses and doctors and that brought me to Iraq, which many may be surprised to learn I enjoyed very much, many times. The Parc meeting was scheduled for lunchtime and I was there to advise on communications. When I got there the woman in charge of internal PR said, "You don't look well at all, are you OK?" And she was right.

I told her I didn't feel very well and that I had pains in my arm. Shortly into the meeting I was called out to take a telephone call, which would have been most unusual. The late Harry Counihan who was Director of Medicine in Baghdad was at the meeting. He was speaking to the College of Surgeons that night but after I returned, full of apologies from taking my phone call, he turned to me with a question.

"Bill, I gather you are not feeling well, would you tell me what the symptoms are?" he asked, looking concerned. I told him and he just got up, picked up the phone and asked for a doctor called John Horgan who was the cardiologist in the old Richmond Hospital. I could hear him on the phone and he said, "John, it's Harry here, I'm bringing down a person to you, he's just starting a heart attack". I was in that hospital for 18 days under the care of Dr Horgan who was the most magnificent cardiologist you could ever meet and the man who, in a very real way, rescued my television career.

He looked after me so well and after a range of scans and tests, told me: "Bill, you are going to need bypass surgery". I didn't want bypasses and was really scared at the idea of heart surgery. He tried to change my mind. "Bypass surgery is like a plumbing job," he told me in his down to earth way and he noted that my heart would be stronger because the imperfections would be eliminated. I still refused the operation but he got me to meet him halfway and agree that if I got any further pains or aches in my chest I'd let him know. And I did. About two months after the initial attack I was brought to the Mater Hospital and surgeon Maurice Nelligan operated and I had my bypasses. One of the consequences of the operation was that I lost an awful lot of confidence and I literally was afraid of my life of pushing myself. I had gone from considering myself indestructible to being in constant fear that the end could come at any moment.

Not surprisingly, I missed that Olympics — it's the only one since 1972 that I didn't host and that meant I missed John Treacy's silver in the marathon, which was a fantastic achievement for the double world cross-country champion. Instead I saw him run his race from a hospital bed. But missing out on being "the star", as Tim O'Connor had put it, had gone from being the most important news I could receive to being the least of my worries. I had my own race to run even though the operations and my time in hospital was up.

At the end of it all, John Horgan came and said to me, "Bill, you have to be very careful in the future," but didn't mean it as I expected. "You have two options," he continued to my surprise. "You can lead a normal life which you should; in fact there is no reason whatsoever why you shouldn't. Or you can become a cardiac cripple which will destroy everything". It was a brutal assessment of the crossroads I found myself at and it stopped me from making the wrong choice and going the wrong way.

I didn't want to go back to television. No matter how hard I had worked to climb the ladder and regardless of the dreams I'd have ever since I walked into the Cork Examiner office as a teenager desperate to become a journalist, this was the end of all that, in my mind. I was sure the stress of television would cause all kinds of trouble and finish me off. But John would have none of it and, metaphorically, led me by the hand, back to television and insisted I get on with life. That was hugely important and I did go back because of him, returning for a World Cup qualifier in Lansdowne Road in 1984.

I admit I was fearful about going back to television and the crew were really worried I could die on screen that evening as they had never come across a presenter who'd had a heart attack and bypasses before! I can only imagine their anxiety but I got through that match, and I was effectively better from that point on. I'd climbed the mountain and could truly enjoy my work again, and I could fully enjoy and appreciate life perhaps for the first time.

The transformation and the confidence I got from returning to television and getting through that first game was reflected in everything else I did thereafter. I was not stupid, mind, and any time I felt I was under any pressure I eased down and paced myself. Like a homing pigeon I went back for medical advice with any problems. But I felt excited by each and every broadcast, and if John Horgan hadn't seen it as his duty to help me back to television, I might have been limping around, packed up work of all sorts and gone on the dole. My father had a couple of heart attacks so maybe it was genetic. But my mended heart would see me through.

That day of the meeting I didn't have a clue what was happening, I thought it was as simple as not feeling well but I haven't the slightest shadow of doubt that the Lord looked after me and put me in a position where someone was there to take care of me straight away. That was also the case when I had my own run in with cancer four years ago too. My two daughters Jill and Sally and Hilary were complaining that I wasn't looking well. And, importantly from their point of view, I was in bad humour and that is not my usual form. They asked me to get a check-up — not with my own GP who is excellent, but they insisted I get the full M.O.T. I agreed and was referred to the Beacon Hospital by Siobhan Weston, a gastroenterologist. Ten days later I was operated on for colon cancer.

There, I was placed under the care of David Fennelly and Jenny Westrop, not just good oncologists but great communicators too. They brought me in and told me precisely what the problem was, precisely what the consequences would be, what the operation would entail, what they expected to be the result, and what would happen afterwards. With all that information, they minimised my fear even though it was cancer and it was the disease that had torn through my family. Facing the operation I didn't worry and they took a cancerous growth out of my colon that I was told was the size of a lemon, and a foot-and-a-half of my intestine while they were at it. They sewed me up and that was it. Somehow it never spread and I've never had a problem since. I know yet again Our Lady was looking after me.

The heart attack initially bothered me and had its effect but that wasn't the case with cancer. Maybe my outlook on life changed in the intervening years and maybe my belief was stronger in later life and that got me through it. Also, I learned to enjoy life that much more and enjoying the panel contributes to this. Unfortunately though, I still have to cut them off as the second half gets underway.

****

Here in television is where I'm visible and known to most

people but Public Relations is my full-time job. It came about, like so many things in my life, by being in the right place at the right time. I was well settled in RTÉ Sport when out of the blue I got an offer I felt I had to consider seriously and most likely couldn't turn down.

Desmond O'Kennedy of OKB and Jack Young, leaders of the Irish advertising industry in the 1970s, decided to set up a public relations company, not because they wanted to invest in a fledgling new industry but because they sought to get advertisers who wanted free publicity off their back. They recalibrated a dormant company, Public Relations of Ireland, now O'Herlihy Communications and asked me to head it up. Their offer was attractive — more money than I was currently earning but, much more important, the owner-ship of the company would be transferred to me after two years. It posed a real dilemma. Should I leave RTÉ Sport where I was doing well or risk my future in an industry about which I knew little and had no practical knowledge or expe-rience. It was not an easy call.

RTÉ Sport under Mick O'Hehir was then predictable in its output but change was beginning as Tim O'Connor, Fred Cogley and Mike Horgan took control of the production output. The days of the Champions League, the Premiership and forensic analysis of big games were still in the distance, but the landscape was changing and sport had the personnel to manage that change dramatically. Today's high standards are a measure of the ability of Tim, in particular, both as an executive and later Group Head of Sport, with imaginative and significant support from Mike and Fred.

I was excited at the prospect of a business career but Hil-ary was not that keen on my leaving RTÉ at that point. She understood my ambition though and was, as always, very supportive. As much as I moved from the Examiner to Newsbeat to 7 Days to sport, they were all progressions within the one industry. With this offer, it made me want to see if I could succeed in a totally different field. While I was mulling over the choice, it kept crossing my mind that I wasn't then challenged in the sports department and I said to myself I wasn't to know if I could make it in business. That pushed me over the edge and I went for it.

I left RTÉ in November 1972 even though there was never any question of my contract not being renewed. Indeed, my next step was staff which was imminent. I was a fully integrated member of the sports team when I left it but I'd say they couldn't have cared less that I changed career paths. O'Connor and Horgan were then the guiding lights of the Sports Department television output and were very good to me. They were worldly wise and extremely cynical individuals. They were great to work with, innovators and pioneers in their approach, but their attitude was if you chose to leave then so be it. Nobody tried to convince me to stay but on the other hand, the notion of people coming in casually to work on TV Sport was still there, so there was no barrier if they wanted me to front a programme now and again. In that sense, it was only a punctuation mark in my journalism career. Or so I thought. As it turned out, it was an age until I returned to this place.

I often feel that there's a resonance with George Lee about this. I remember about eight months into my PR career I was feeling sorry for myself, thinking I had made a big mistake in leaving RTÉ. I was working slavishly hard to grow my company and was in the office at eight o'clock in the morning and still there at eight o'clock at night because I was establishing it. It was a tough grind and getting clients was hard work and while those hours are fine when you enjoy something, this wasn't then the case with me.

Working in public relations was a huge learning experience. As a capable journalist my initial assumption was that it was about media but that was very much a limited perspective. I had never been close to business and it was only now I began to understand business planning and strategy and the importance of dealing with all stakeholders to advance a company's objectives and improve the bottom line. It was a real eye-opener to me but not to those today entering a very changed industry which makes a major contribution to business development.

Back in 1972 I was approached simply because I was a journalist. Jack Young was the person I dealt with mainly and he would have seen me in a very simplistic sense. He didn't know me personally but I had a relatively good reputation, would have been seen regularly on current affairs and sport doing a good job. They saw me as an option and that was it, not some great businessman. It was just about picking a journalist who could run the show and get advertisers off their back.

We had good clients including Coca-Cola and Beecham and many others but I was not happy. I remember one morning at 7am before I left home. I was staring out the window and said to Hilary, "What in God's name have I done?" She told me if I was that unhappy, which I most certainly was, I should stop sulking and do something about it. Her suggestion was go back to RTÉ, explain the situation and how I felt, and see what was available. It was great advice.

In a way I had become a television animal. I always saw myself as a journalist who worked in television and I made that sharp distinction, but I had become a television animal without even knowing it. I suspect that's part of what prompted George Lee to leave politics. No matter what business you go into after television, there is a huge sense of loss and a feeling there's something missing from your life. I'd love to have spoken to George and if I had that chance, I'd have told him you cannot make a judgment after eight months. I learnt that the hard way.

Following Hilary's advice, I went to see RTÉ's Controller of Programmes, Michael Garvey. I had a long conversation with him about where I was and how unhappy I was. He listened sympathetically, made some constructive suggestions, and then said to me, "I don't understand you at all. You have your own business, you have good clients, and you have the potential to make a lot of money and make a good career out of public relations. And you want to come back here? All you are going to be is a down-the-line reporter in the Sports Department and you want to change a potentially very good career for that. I think you are completely crazy, Bill".

He continued. "OK, I'll tell you what I'll do. I don't have a job now and I think you'd be very silly to take one if I had, so we will give it another year and if you feel exactly like you do now one year from today, we'll talk about having your job back." I went out, at once relieved and exhilarated and said to myself, "They still want me." It was a profoundly important meeting. Michael was clearly a good psychologist as well as a good broadcaster and he settled me down. The weight of leaving RTÉ seemed to have lifted and I carried on, with renewed vigour, building my public relations business which is now managed by my daughter Jill.

Increasingly, I adapted to my new industry and learned the skill of communicating at so many different levels. Perhaps it was my growing role in public relations mixed with my current affairs background, but by 1977 it opened political doors as well. I maintained my friendship with my '7 Days' mate Ted Nealon and when he was invited, because of his strong political base, to play in an Oireachtas golf out-ing he asked me to join him. But he didn't last the 18 holes as he was invited to meet Conor Cruise O'Brien, Minister for Posts and Telegraphs, in Leinster House as a matter of urgency. Ted would not say why in advance but when he returned he told me he was offered the job of Government Press Secretary. Poacher turned gamekeeper, eh, Ted? He was a highly respected political correspondent and I, like others, welcomed his appointment enthusiastically.

I always had a huge respect for Ted. Strategically, he was impressive, his media judgement and contacts were top class and most of all he never pretended to have knowledge or skills he did not have. It was that sense that led to his establishing an expert group to advise on all aspects of communications. Ted was and is a close friend of Enda Marren, the lawyer and important Fine Gael activist who is today Chairman of the party's trustees. Both worked together to establish the group and Enda, who had a great capacity to identify talent, brought in people like myself, Pat Heneghan, Joe Jennings, Shane Molloy and Frank Flannery to assist in communication of the policies of the Fine Gael–Labour Government under Garret FitzGerald.

We were, allegedly, the National Handlers — not a title we had in mind but one established and promoted by John Healy in a sarcastic, pejorative bid to destabilise us. Fianna Fáil jumped on the Healy bandwagon. We were, they said with a straight face, a group of unelected people making Government policy. Rubbish. We were nothing of the kind.

We were advisors, under the Official Secrets Act, who evaluated from our different streams of expertise what the reaction would be to proposed Government policies, how such actions would be perceived by different sections of society and what might the benefits be. When briefed we would evaluate, come back with reaction and presentational ideas –

but never reveal outside of the group what was proposed by Government.

Were we resented? Yes, both by Government supporters and opposition but this was because, like so many, they swallowed the John Healy line. In the greater scheme of Government we were small fries and we knew it but I was delighted to be involved. It was a hugely important era in Irish politics and Garret FitzGerald was an immensely popular figure at a time when the country longed for a good, decent, patriotic leader who would lead us out of the excesses of the Haughey and TACA eras. FitzGerald attracted many thousands into Fine Gael through his values and he transformed Fine Gael politics by translating Declan Costello's 'Just Society' into party policy.

The so-called National Handlers, for all the publicity, were very much at the edge, not the centre, of Government. I make no claims to have been in the inner circle of advisors, because I was not, but I had a specific role in radio and developing efficient and effective television communications.

Dealing with Garret was not always easy because he had an intellectual strength which was formidable. I remember rewriting a speech for him, from which I eliminated so many of the sub-clauses he loved on the basis it would make a better soundbite. But I got blown out of the water for my troubles. My rewrite damaged the substance of the script, in his mind, and so was rejected out of hand. Sub-clauses restored! Garret, though, was well able to take advice and he appreciated my TV and radio skills. I discussed his media coverage with him and the importance of sharp, direct contact with the people and suggested he would benefit from media training.

He agreed. I suggested, to the astonishment of many, the training should be undertaken by Bunny Carr. "Are you mad," people said to me, "Bunny Carr. Quicksilver. Why are you using him?" Quite a campaign to change the trainer ensued. I would not budge. I had always admired Bunny's use of television, his ease in contacting his audience, his comfort in presenting. As far as I was concerned he was the man and it had to be Bunny, no-one else.

Bunny proved me right as I knew he would. Garret went to him to prepare for an important television interview and Bunny gave him such a tough grilling I felt he was a loss to RTÉ's current affairs. Garret was delighted with the training that evening and went back for a number of other sessions in which Bunny covered all the issues and areas likely to be part of future dealings with the broadcast media. This, in effect, was the beginning of Carr Communications' role in political training.

My role in politics has lessened through the years but I was lucky enough to work for a short period with Enda Kenny when he was Minister for Tourism. Enda impressed me greatly with his commitment to promoting Ireland and one small example stands out. He watched Dublin's St Patrick's Day parade and was appalled by its lack of imagination. The Dublin parade, he said, should be the best in the world and he ordered a complete rethink, appointed an artistic director and said he wanted a parade that Ireland could be proud of within a year. It was delivered.

I always thought Enda was completely underestimated and was, frankly, shocked by the superficial nature of the media evaluation of him as Leader of the Opposition. Enda has warmth, personality, passion – and steel. In a series of radio interviews which I did in the months before the last General Election I made it clear that there had been a huge misjudgement of the man and the election would prove it.

Enda, you will remember, was being battered by criticism

and he was grateful that I was so positive in my interviews which were essentially about sport but strayed into politics because of my background. He rang me to thank me for my very public support when so many were keeping their heads down.

He didn't forget, either. Hilary and I were about to sit down to watch Leinster in the Heineken Cup final when the phone rang. It was Enda. After a couple of pleasantries he said: "I'm ringing to ask what you're doing on Monday?"

"I'm delighted to tell you I'm playing golf with the Dublin journalists Golf Society at Killeen Castle and very much looking forward to it, " I replied.

"That's a pity. I was hoping you would be free because I wanted to invite you as my guest to meet President Obama when he comes to town," said Enda.

"You can consider the golf cancelled," I told him, "I am delighted to accept your invitation!"

Meeting President Obama and his lovely wife Michelle was a very special moment even if it had been very rushed. During brief conversations with President Obama and Michelle they both revealed that they were delighted with their short visit and when leaving Michelle said, "We're so sorry it's such a short visit. We will definitely come back to Ireland."

****

As for my own company it grew over the years and I'm grateful I stuck with it after those early days and doubts. But being a television presenter was never an advantage in terms of promoting my public relations business and, in keeping both aspects of my career separate, I never used it as such. This, I now admit, was probably a mistake.

A remarkable thing about sports broadcasting is that you

can be a superb professional, take on the English channels and beat them hands down on audience numbers week on week, something no other Irish television productions are obliged to do, yet be dismissed as somewhat trivial for all that. There's a sharp distinction drawn between business and sport and the fundamental aspect of professionalism, both editorially and presentationally, is ignored. Is it our own fault? Perhaps, but I would have to say in my own case being a television sports anchor did not help promote my business. But there are many other elements too, like not being clubby, being slightly anti-social in terms of networking and coming to Dublin later in life than most. Perhaps I assumed, because I was on television, people would come knocking on my door. Some did, but not so many, and I didn't pursue others hard enough. If I seek a fool's pardon it would be that when I finish a day's work in my PR business I'm here in RTÉ Sport while others are perhaps networking.

But in developing my PR business, O'Herlihy Communications has been at the cutting edge of some of the nation's major developments including the introduction of the Luas concept to Dublin — an awareness campaign described by the judge presiding over the public inquiry into its viability, as outstanding; the translation of Irish Permanent from a building society to a PLC — a first in Irish financial history; the development of Waterford Crystal's marketing; managing media relations for the 3 Irish Golf Championship and the first stage of the World Rally Championship; building the profile of the Irish Sports Council from its inception; promoting the Combat Poverty Agency; managing media and crisis management for McDonalds fast-food restaurants; and developing a strong campaign against illegal cigarette smuggling into Ireland. Overall, I'm proud O'Herlihy Communications has won 15 Public Relations Consultants

Association awards and commendations for excellence in communications — recognition by the Irish public relations industry, north and south, of the consistent high standard of our work.

It's not all been roses, of course. Back in 2004 the Sunday Independent reported I had lobbied the Irish Government on behalf of the Irish company Bula Resources to lift sanctions on Iraq. It was an example of a newspaper using names, mine and Albert Reynolds, to sell the thinnest of stories. I arranged a number of meetings for a client which I did not attend and there was never any question of my promoting Saddam Hussein or supporting the government of Iraq. Indeed any such suggestion was nonsense.

I also worked for Michael Lowry when in Government when he was Minister for Communications and enjoyed every moment. Lowry was tough, smart and decisive with no tolerance for verbiage or waffling but he was warm and a pleasure to work with. He was politically astute and was principally responsible for John Bruton becoming Taoiseach through a transfer of power rather than a general election. I never saw anything corrupt in his dealings during his time in Government and that includes the awarding of the mobile phone licence to Denis O'Brien's company.

I remember in the early days of mobile phone submissions asking Lowry if he would have an influence on who might get it. "You must be joking," he said, "this will go all the way to Brussels and if there is any sign of political interference I'll be sacked." How ironic in the light of later events. I can't imagine Lowry's writ ran deep enough in the department to deliver any verdict. In fact, I was told subsequently by Lowry's departmental advisors that O'Brien's submission was the best by far and that he deservedly was awarded the licence. I speak now only of my contacts with Lowry in the

Department, but I support Lowry in his belief that the tribunal treated him harshly about the licence. I never saw signs of any wrongdoing and indeed I can testify to his refusal to respond to certain requests for ministerial favours because he thought they were inappropriate.

His dealings with Ben Dunne were a different matter, something outside the scope of my work for the department. How Lowry and Dunne arranged payment for refrigeration services was a private matter but when the details of a tax avoidance story broke it was only a matter of hours before he was forced to resign. So many took the high moral ground and raged against Lowry's action but I had certain sympathy. "If you're a sole trader and the client wants to pay you a certain way it can place you in a very difficult situation," he told me. How right — it cost him his Ministry, his role in Fine Gael but not his seat and it robbed Fine Gael of one of their shrewdest political operators. He wasn't one to stand for any rubbish.

Just like the lads here in Studio 4. Having cut through the action of the first half I hand back to George Hamilton for the second half. We've been serious and responsible for 15 minutes but that offers no guarantees for the next 45 minutes off screen.

CHAPTER 6

Revolution And Evolution

The second half kicks off and, for the moment, the game itself remains as background noise as Dunphy is more concerned about Brady's sunburn. It's a continuation from a conversation that started long before the show and he's not letting it go. It's probably because he sensed he was getting somewhere a few hours back and now that he has time on his hands, he doesn't want to miss out on the opportunity to get a reaction.

Until the banter, it was peace and quiet around here. At 5.30pm, I went upstairs to meet with editor Eugene O'Neill and passed through the sports department where they've painted on the wall the phrase "Okey dokey" amongst some other more storied lines that have been said on air across the generations. I'm honoured to be placed alongside some of the legends that have graced this place but in this business you are only as good as your last broadcast and it's why on a sofa upstairs we went through exactly what would be happening tonight, even if we've gone through it all for other games a thousand times before.

Eugene gave me Giles' column from the *Evening Herald* but more importantly a draft script reflecting the production outline. With that in hand, we prepared for every small intricacy from the length of ad breaks to how everything would be rejigged if extra-time were to happen. He's so thorough that the plan went over 40 pages with every insert and every eventuality carefully noted. Indeed, having scanned through it all, I felt completely comfortable and sensed nothing could go wrong. With that in mind, we headed for our meeting room, he ordered some food to keep him going for the long night ahead, but before long, bouncing down the corridor I could hear the voices of the panellists as they arrived. Once that happens, you know you're not far from the off and you're at the final hurdle before the show begins.

When Giles saw Eugene's food, he wanted some for himself and had the runner arrange to bring it from the canteen. Next in was Brady, and then Dunphy who immediately started slagging him about his red face. Brady's response was that it was because of high blood pressure which he said wasn't helped by being anywhere near Dunphy.

Each was given cuttings from the Press Association, the *Guardian* and a press pack but were more concerned with one another. They'd most certainly done their research in their own time anyway, and besides, they are never very far from what's happening in football. "There's the Grand Marshal," Dunphy said of Giles, referring to his role in the St Patrick's Day parade. Thereafter the conversation remained largely casual as these days we aren't usually on the air until 7.30pm whereas in the old days when it was a 7pm start there was much more time to fill and preparation to do.

In fact it was so casual that when Giles' food arrived, Brady's biggest concern was his own meal and again the runner was sent off across the grounds, this time in search of a fry with which he returned, totally out of breath. "And you whinging about blood pressure," noted Dunphy, jumping in with two feet. "If that's true, it's not me, it's that crap you're eating. But, hey, give me a sausage?" It wasn't so much a question as he reached over and grabbed one. "Yep, cholesterol, nothing but grease there," he said to Brady.

Eugene quickly steered the meeting back towards its purpose. "I sent you through some stuff last night, didn't I, Bill? So we might get on the air a minute or two early tonight if horse-racing finishes early." I'd already planned for that and try to engage the rest of the lads and get them focused in on me and my questions good and early. "Yeah, the racing, it's gone badly for the Irish hasn't it?"

"It doesn't matter to me where the winners come from Bill," said Dunphy. "I couldn't care if he's Japanese as long as I've backed him. Would you care, Liam, if you back a 10-1 Japanese winner?"

From there the talk was all over the place. I started to chat to Giles about the Premier League. Dunphy pulled matters back to betting. Brady was more focussed on his rashers at that stage until Head of Sport Ryle Nugent came in to say a quick hello. "I want to make a complaint," joked Brady, before he was even in the door. "Eugene gets serviettes and the rest of us..."

"I'm surprised you don't have that in your contract," laughed Dunphy. "Quick, Ryle, get a pen, he wants a sub-clause in his contract — serviettes on arrival."

But Ryle, a terrific Head of Sport, was, and is, well able for it and his opening words were about Brady's sunburn too. "Were you off playing golf?" he asks. But of course it was Dunphy who answered. "Damn sure. Isn't the head roasted off him? You look like a bloke who was playing golf on a windy day. Barbados was it? In this economy? You need to be changing more about Brady's contract than the serviettes, Ryle." Dunphy was in his element.

"That was three months ago," muttered Brady matter-offactly.

And it's that conversation Dunphy has returned to now as if there's been no passing of time in between. "Billo said you were in Barbados just two weeks ago, didn't you, Bill? Not three months ago." Even Brady takes a second to realise just what he's talking about but largely ignores him. This is the kind of carry-on which a lot of other analysts we've had over the years were surprised by and they took time to adjust. They'd usually arrive from the conservatism of English soccer coverage where they were limited in what they could say on the air and how much time they had to say it. Here they found it the opposite, although most embraced it and loved it after the initial surprise. It's helped them improve their own talents, too, in their performances across the water.

Graeme Souness is very much a case in point. At the end of the last World Cup, I said to him, "I enjoy working with you, you add enormously to the programme because you've got so much to say. You say it very well and you are very trenchant in your comments when required. But can I say this to you? I don't see that on Sky at all. I listen to you and to me you are completely bland." He wasn't taken aback at all; in fact he wasn't even surprised. "It's interesting you should say that, my wife says exactly the same."

"So why don't you change?" I asked. And I think he has changed. He is much tougher, more insightful, and I think he has a foil now in Gary Neville more so than Jamie Redknapp who is that worst combination of nice, boring and safe. Souness is far better and I'd like to think we can take credit for that as he learned a lot from his time with us.

When he did his first World Cup here back in 2006, a lot of people objected. So at the end of the tournament, I said on air, "Now Graeme, it's been a pleasure working with you, but I have to say something. I'm sure you will be surprised to learn the number of people, when they heard you were coming on the programme, that objected to you on two grounds. First of all, Rangers. But far more importantly, you are perceived to be anti-Irish due to the way you have treated Irish players." "Anti-Irish?" he replied, astonished. "How could I be anti-Irish, isn't my wife Dickie Rock's first cousin." It was a home run. More and more people liked him from that point onwards.

In his early appearances, he regarded our programme as the Dunphy and Giles show. Sometimes, he was clearly holding back and when I told him to get more involved he said he didn't want to be intruding too much. I had to tell him that's why he was there but he changed and became much tougher. A big part of growing on the air might have been the fact he felt more comfortable off the air too. Dunphy used to admire him as a player but thought he had a big ego. However they started to get on well during that tournament and Dunphy liked to set him up. He used to convince the women in make-up that "there's a guy coming up shortly, he's a fine thing, but he's a bit insecure so make a fuss over him, just to build up his confidence a bit before the show". Insecure was the last thing Souness was and Dunphy would hang around outside the door to see how he'd react to all the attention.

At the beginning of the coverage, Souness admitted to me that he felt a little out of his depth. Giles had played against him and said he wasn't just good; he was, in fact, great. He was hard but he could play when he wanted, was a leader and a driver of a remarkable Liverpool team. That resulted in presence and credibility but it wasn't being translated onto the air and there's only so far a playing reputation will get you in this business. When he realised what we were about though, he tried harder and often with great humour. Talking about great players one night he said to Giles, "I remember you well, you were a great player" Then he turned to Dunphy and said "so where did *you* play?"

The fact he upped his game meant a lot to the lads, myself and everyone involved as it showed that he cared not just about his work but the reputation of the programme.

Dietmar Hamann is a tournament regular for us here too and he was a hit from the start. He'd had several well documented gambling issues and I'm told at his lowest point had lost hundreds of thousands in a day. But Brady and Dunphy wouldn't be men for skirting around the issue; they love their horse-racing and his presence wasn't going to stop them. When they came into studio and saw Hamann there, they continued to natter away about this race and that. No matter what it was, and no matter how obscure, Dietmar would tell them who won straight away. They loved that and he had a great sense of humour and wouldn't ever sit on the fence. They were ideal traits for this programme.

Then there was Ossie Ardiles, a nice guy, down-to-earth, humble and a football great. But I found him hard to understand at times and so did the audience. Talking to him face to face wasn't too bad but when you gave him something to voice over, for instance if he was to talk you through a goal, he was speaking his very special kind of English. The trouble was I didn't want to be rude by saying, "I don't know what on earth you are talking about". I relied on the tried and trusted formula and followed up his comment with a "what-you-are-really-saying-is-this" reaction. In other words get him to repeat his comment so at least people might more clearly grasp what he was on about.

Of course he was really good on the game, having been a top class player with insight and knowledge. It was a measure of his status that when he had his testimonial Diego Maradona turned up and played in it. Ossie really respected the older Argentinian players and looked up to them despite what he had achieved himself. He was great fun off camera and a particularly close friend of Liam's.

Giles actually played against Ossie during his time with Shamrock Rovers. Prior to the 1978 World Cup, a League of Ireland selection went to South America for what they thought was an exhibition match. When they got there, they found out it was billed as an international and the opposition was enriched with stars. Suddenly they found themselves up against this great team, which included nine of the starters that would win the World Cup months later, in a packed La Bombonera and were 3-0 down by the break. The fear was it would be six or seven until they got an amazing goal back after the restart, after which both sides stopped playing at full tilt. It was a miracle result and the two of them reminisced about it.

Despite his English language limitations as a pundit, Ardiles was popular and at the same time his presence was a measure of the ambition of RTÉ. For many, he might not be the most easily understood guy, but it showed how advanced RTÉ had become in their soccer coverage and their ambitions. In that sense, there has been evolutionary development in RTÉ soccer and that's why we always stay on top of the pile in domestic coverage.

As good as Eugene has been in taking the show forward, so many of the foundations were laid by Tim O'Connor and Mike Horgan. If Eugene is a pacifier, Tim was the opposite and was never afraid of being confrontational. He backed away from nothing and shied away from no-one. At one stage a reporter confined mainly to radio complained to Tim about his limited television opportunities. The response was brief and savage. "As long as I am Head of Sport, you will not be on television because you have the kind of face that could give nightmares to small children so you will not broadcast on television." When Tim was firm, he was completely firm.

He took over the role of Head of Sport after Fred Cogley, who at one stage was looking at other options. I was at the Irish Golf Writers' dinner one night and I met Fred, for whom I always had a very high regard as he is one of the most decent and genuine people you would ever meet. I asked how he was and he said he was giving up his job as Head of Sport. "What are you doing instead?," I asked and he said he was going to be a specialist rugby commentator and RTÉ had committed to giving him carte blanche to cover rugby anywhere in the world. In other words if he wanted to cover South Africa versus the All Blacks in Cape Town he'd go off and do so. But another very important point, he was told he could also present whatever programmes he wanted.

I said to him, "Two things, Fred. That's complete nonsense. If I was editor of a programme and wanted Bill O'Herlihy or whoever to do it and was told I have to take Fred Cogley, I'd say no and that's that. You will find yourself in a complete limbo. People may want you but they may have their own plans and their own agenda. And secondly, from your point of view, they won't be sending you to Cape Town and Melbourne and Christchurch to do matches that few give a damn about in Ireland. This is crazy stuff. You told me once that if you were offered the Director General's job, you wouldn't under any circumstances leave the role of Head of Sport because it was the best job in the world. And now you are giving it up voluntarily? Fred, I'm sorry for saying this but, as a friend, I think you are making a mistake."

I got a phone call the following morning, asking would I meet him for lunch. He had planned to come in to RTÉ at 2.30pm to resign his role, sign a new contract and move on but he changed his mind. He said he had taken my reaction very seriously, reflected on what I said and thought I was correct. He wanted advice on how he would deal with RTÉ, and he then worked out a strategy for the new scenario. Instead of going in to sign something they thought was a fait accompli, he went in and said he had changed his mind and was staying as Head of Sport. The reaction was less than joyous as their intention had been to install Tim O'Connor in his place with Fred doing a different job. Fred remained as Head of Sport but his functions were divided and Tim O'Connor was given a major role in determining the future direction of RTÉ Sport. Tim took over the function of concluding contracts with sports bodies and more importantly bringing in the new product which would change radically the sports output and Fred concentrated on the more traditional elements of the job. When Fred finally did retire, Tim was automatically moved into his position.

I had an enormous regard for Tim. He was supportive, extremely fair and good but so tough when the occasion demanded. I remember once when Dunphy on air was critical of George Hamilton for some comment he made in his commentary. It was not on, you do not say something critical of your own commentator and I deemed it to be out of order. Indeed, we had a row during the commercial break and I told Dunphy that having a go at George on air was poor form. He said, "If you come back and ask me any questions about this I am going to go back in much harder". So I said nothing, asked no more questions on the issue and that was the end of it as far as I was concerned.

Tim was out of the country but by Saturday morning, I was on the first tee at Foxrock Golf Club when the phone rang. He said, "I was watching the tape of the other night and I am not one bit pleased that you didn't pursue Dunphy". I tried to explain the reason and said I felt if I went after him, he would have come out with much worse and it would have been a pyrrhic victory — and bad for him, bad for George and definitely bad for RTÉ. "Well I wasn't impressed and I'll tell you one thing, if you feel you can't take Dunphy on in an area where he was clearly wrong, I will replace you on the programme, just be aware of that". It was the only time he said that to me but Tim was serious. He demanded standards.

When I first met them, he and Mike Horgan lived a lifestyle that I found to be astonishing. They were good time charlies, frequented the 'in' places around Dublin, had, as far as I could tell, a Bohemian lifestyle and unbelievable stamina day after day, night after night and yet they were able to do their jobs extremely well. The first time I ever saw Tim in action in a way that impressed me, though, was at an NUJ chapel meeting in RTÉ and he did a brilliant presentation in opposition to the organisation's proposals of the day. He had an intellectual ability, and a power of persuasion, which I had never seen in the casual conversations we had had.

When he got into a power position he was strong in his observations. He was rarely unfair but never shirked what had to be said. If you weren't delivering, you were told straight off and had to get your act together. One of the best things about him was that he was always available to talk, to discuss, to help and he had a marvellous sense of the absurd which gave us all so many laughs. Tim's insights were fascinating too and I remember him telling me one time that his experience of people in the frontline of broadcasting sport suggested they were all insecure and he considered me insecure as well. He thought people like me in a broadcasting role were personally shy yet seemed to disprove this point in our public roles.

144

As for Mike, he created RTÉ's soccer panel and demanded it be honest and forthright and strong in its views. For these reasons it's been successful and has the ability to attract some of the biggest names in world soccer. But let's have no doubt, that success and those traits are down to the lads beside me rather than any big names that come in for major tournaments.

I glance over at them. "Does it sting?," asks Dunphy again looking at the sunburn. Brady just sighs and looks on at the game.

****

With my public relations company going well and establishing a strong reputation from the late 1970s, other things started to go well too. More and more I was called on by Tim O'Connor and Mike Horgan to work with the sports department. I presented rugby initially and was anchor for the 1987 World Cup and I presented a very good programme called 'Rugby After Dark' where Mick Doyle was the main man and Tony Ward began making his media reputation on it. I did the first 'The Sunday Game' programmes for a couple of years, where I was the analyst and Jim Carney was the presenter before Michael Lyster came on board. But it's soccer I've been most identified with, even if we stuttered along for a time after the panel expanded to incorporate Giles for the 1986 World Cup.

Surprisingly, those struggles included Euro '88. Giles was on duty but Dunphy was sitting at home watching it on television because he'd told Tim he wanted more money and refused to work unless he got it. Before the previous major tournament he had given another ultimatum and said that if Giles wasn't on the panel he wouldn't do it. It wasn't resolved

WE'LL LEAVE IT THERE SO: THE BILL O'HERLIHY STORY

on that occasion until the 11th hour when Tim went to his house and said he'd go for it but it would be on Dunphy's head if it all went wrong. At that stage Dunphy was a sportswriter in the *Sunday Tribune* and, later, *Sunday Independent* so wasn't stuck for money but O'Connor had given in once and wouldn't again. Thus, in 1988, Dunphy was out in the cold and as good as Giles was, that hurt us a little.

Even if Ireland did well there, the coverage never really took off. Giles was in an awkward position because he had been in for the national job when Jack Charlton got it. He's told me since that people thought his comments on Ireland were biased against Jack out of bitterness, when the truth was he was giving an honest opinion and it took people time to realise that. There were those who said Giles should have been more determined going for the Irish job and that he had chickened out to an extent. In fact he said to me if he wanted it, he'd have canvassed for it and Jack getting in the way was actually a relief because it gave him an excuse to back off.

It wasn't until Italia '90 that we began to realise how big the soccer panel would become. Ireland's first World Cup transformed the place of soccer in our society, and from our perspective it transformed how it was viewed as well. Up to that point, it had always been a poor relation to Gaelic games and rugby just as RTÉ was always seen as the poor relation to cross-channel coverage. We were losing on all fronts.

It's strange now knowing how many hundreds of thousands of people will be tuning in tonight, to reflect that before that World Cup we rarely made an impact when it came to ratings. In a way we were like Jimmy Magee and people don't, perhaps, understand the difficult role he has had in Irish broadcasting. Way back then, everyone saw BBC and ITV as the definitive sports channels with the best commentators, the slickest presenters and the most knowledgeable analysts. That was the way it always had been perceived and that was the environment that Jimmy was thrust into. Indeed, it took quite some time for people to realise how good he was and he had a hard time establishing his commentary persona in competition with the likes of Kenneth Wolstenholme. Familiarity bred devotion and loyalty in his case.

BBC is an outstanding television service and its top stars were idolised. Then the Irish attitude was that someone abroad was a bigger expert than anyone at home; the BBC culture had been embedded into the system and people would ask "Why watch Jimmy?" since English coverage was the be-all. In terms of our studio panel, we were in a similar situation to Jimmy and in the same way, the public initially asked "why watch us?" Then came Italia '90 though and the most loved Irish side of them all, and people wanted nothing but Ireland — team and television. They changed channels and stayed with RTÉ. We were blunt, exciting and different. It wasn't always to everyone's liking since a lot of people wanted us to be fans with typewriters in a manner of speaking. Some considered us to be out of step with the public mood at times, but there was huge interest in what we said. That has maintained itself to today.

RTÉ frequently beats English TV channels in audience terms by a factor of 10 to one because of the forthright nature of the comment. The Irish audience is more sophisticated, better educated and definitely more perceptive than those in the UK. If they are being fed drivel or bland rubbish in Ireland they see it for what it is and won't take it. But if they are given honest comment, even though they might not necessarily like it, they will realise it is honest. In fact I'm told that when you go into some pubs, not just in Ireland, there would be talk through the match coverage yet there would be dead silence when we come on. That's a measure of how much the lads have gotten inside the Irish psyche but their first chance wasn't until our first World Cup and they made the most of it. After that they had a special place in Irish sport.

Not that it was easy, especially given Jack Charlton's attitude when it came to dealing with us. His audience was very much on his mind and I can remember interviewing him for a special Christmas TV programme after Italia '90. The programme was based on a 60-minute interview with inserts. It was motoring along and after about 15 minutes I asked what I thought was a relatively straightforward and simple follow-up question. I was wrong.

"Stop the interview," Jack shouted.

"Why?" I said, confused, surprised and taken aback.

"You are trying to set me up with the English media."

"I am doing no such thing," I said, "I am simply following up what you said."

"You are setting me up with the English media and I will not have it. You have two options now, we can stop and start again and you won't try that again. Or I'll walk out."

"I don't know what you are talking about Jack."

"You are setting me up."

He was so sensitive about the English media. Giles told me just how bad he was when it came to journalists across the channel and how defensive he became. I guess I asked the wrong supplementary, but it wasn't just that instance — I always found him hard to deal with as a journalist. I wasn't a fan of his because I felt, putting it politely, he did very offhand interviews with us. Ger Canning, for instance, was a post-match reporter and got a horrible time from Jack who was offhand towards him on many occasion for no reason at all. Then a BBC or ITV reporter would come along and

Standing outside RTE HQ, the place where I have seen so many of my journalistic dreams come to fruition

With my mum and dad at Jill's First Holy Communion day in 1983 and (below) with old pal Mike Murphy off the Queensland coast while filming 'Murphy's Australia' in 1991 –what a tough job!

On my wedding day with Hilary, November 7, 1970

Being the proud father of the bride at my daughter Sally's wedding to Paddy; and (below) Sally, Hilary and myself at Jill's wedding to John Ryan

I love this picture.... just Jill and me

The entire clan... Jill and her husband John, Hilary and myself, Sally and husband Paddy and grandchildren Martha, Bill, Jack and Isla and (below) enjoying our wedding anniversary with family

With Jill and Sally celebrating my 70th birthday in September 2008 and (below) Hilary's mum 'Tom' with Jill and Sally on Jill's fifth birthday

Taking it easy with my little grandson Jack

All pictures courtesy of: Finbarr O'Rourke, The RTÉ Picture Library and Barry Moore/Photogenic.ie

suddenly all would change and his mood would lighten. Giles noted it on air more than once. "I see Jack has been at the charm school again," he told our audience. But if I had it hard with him as did Canning, then Dunphy was in a different league altogether and his clashes with Charlton at that World Cup were one of the reasons everyone tuned in. It may have been a sideshow but had it been any other time those two would have been the main event — it got that big.

As far as Giles and Dunphy were concerned, Ireland had a great team and many would make the argument that it was the greatest Irish team ever. By any measurement, we had a group of real stars and the studio judgment was that Jack never permitted them to play as they were capable of playing. Like Giovanni Trapattoni now, he had a system they had to play to and Kevin Moran told me afterwards that they hated it though they recognised how effective it was. Giles and Dunphy had a very different view, a belief that had the players been allowed the liberty to play as they could, we could have done extremely well. In fact they would have been of the view we had a good chance of winning that World Cup.

I tended to agree. There was no reason why we couldn't have had the same strong defence but been allowed play going forward. Instead though, the team were forced to conform to a pattern which exhausted guys like John Aldridge who spent 90 minutes defending as much as attacking. The problem was people got swept away by Jack's populist tactics and couldn't see it for what it really was which was restrictive.

Nowadays, many footballers will tell you that they believe Jack did huge damage to the Irish game in a football sense. It's important to recognise he popularised the game in a way that had never happened before and he brought soccer to the forefront of Irish sport where it had never been. He transformed the whole landscape. These were the positives but the flipside was — and ex-players say this off the record to us when they come in for an appearance — Jack damaged soccer here because he was so negative. What he was doing translated to the Phoenix Park and various grounds around Ireland and inhibited the development of the game and Dunphy and Giles were conscious of this at the time. That was the source of the row and the famous incident with the biro after the Egypt game.

"I felt embarrassed for soccer," said Dunphy when we came back to the studio after the scoreless draw. "I felt embarrassed for all the good players and for our great tradition in soccer. This is nothing to do with the players who played today, because this is a good side. But I feel embarrassed and ashamed by that performance; everyone in the country has been let down. Most people won't understand, you have to know the game a little bit or have played the game a little bit. Guys who play amateur soccer will know. The Egyptians were terrible, are terrible, and England will do a job on them. We should be ashamed by the way we went about the game. Ashamed and embarrassed."

"Would you go as strongly as that?" I asked Giles but Dunphy interrupted. "John never goes as strongly as me. All the great players we produced, this is a great footballing country, and to be playing that rubbish..." He rhymed off a few past players at that point and while people remember him throwing the biro across the room, I'm not sure that was a conscious thing. He hopped it on the desk and leaned back. But over in Italy, Jack was told Dunphy said he was ashamed to be Irish which of course wasn't true. That was a mischievous interpretation of his rant. Days later because of all the complaints from those who misunderstood, we had to address the issue again, play the clip again, clear the air and move on.

It was chaos on a level we had not seen before.

Giles escaped the sound and the fury even though he had been just as critical, although his wording had been less strident and more sensitive. But he agreed completely with Dunphy and felt an obligation to call it as he saw it because he was remembering his own playing days and the importance of establishing a style of play which would translate right through the system. He had very definite views on what constituted greatness and had little time for players being lauded as great that he thought never really were. He called them television players like Glenn Hoddle or Rodney Marsh, whereas he considered John Robertson of Nottingham Forest to have been truly great without ever getting the credit. He hated superficial judgement and wanted to make clear his philosophy now he was on television. Thus he didn't hold back when it came to our group games in Italy. It's not that we never praised Jack either but we all knew that our job was to be straight, give credit where it was due, criticism where it was deserved but overall maintain balance.

Charlton and Giles had played together at Leeds and had very different philosophies on how the game should be played even then. Jack used to think Giles came back too far for the ball and was too deep and Giles would say he had to because it wasn't being given to him up the pitch. Off the field it was a different story and they liked one another but by the World Cup, Giles made it his policy not to talk to him and keep well clear of him, on the grounds that it's better to keep your distance from players and games you are commenting on in order to be free to be critical. And there was no shortage of criticism around that World Cup. The team was much, much better than Jack allowed it to be and in fact Giles argued that he would never have gotten into that Irish team, such were the restrictions on its playing style.

Brady was working for the BBC at that stage, was based in Italy and he too was steering well clear of Jack. When he became a part of our panel he told me that he was picked to play against West Germany in a friendly in 1989, was taken off after 35 minutes and was adamant that he was put on just so he could be taken off. He, apparently, had a major row with Jack over that. He was fuming, he thought Jack had humiliated him, that his skills were not appreciated and were not wanted. They subsequently made up but Jack's action hurt Brady a lot.

Brady also said to us he was happy to have the television gig as he was quickly figuring out minute by minute he wouldn't have played much had he been in the squad and he'd have hated being stuck there for a month with a manager who had no time for him, listening to criticism from back home. However, he did also tell us later on that while the Irish players were initially taken aback by Dunphy's forthright attitude, they were used to him by then.

It's important to recognise we were desperate for Ireland to succeed playing well but we were there for a particular function which was to analyse the game to the best of our knowledge. There was no point in playing the populist line and making a silk purse out of a sow's ear. That was the view of Giles and Dunphy and they were not going to do that even if they were perceived to be party poopers or much worse. Nobody likes rigorous criticism but from our perspective our job was to inform and engage the soccer fan. The real core audience when we started was the football lover who was part of a small group because the Irish soccer community was almost a ghetto audience. Dunphy used to say, "Rugby is for toffs and GAA is for culchies" and his idea was to get the hardcore soccer fan to tune in and build on that.

In order to make that happen our plan was to be like a

group of people watching a match and talking as if there were no cameras there. People were addicted. Since then Dunphy has done some work for BBC and ITV and noted that as soon as the lights and cameras were off in studio, guys only then started saying what they really thought. We were different and at the beginning some Irish fans couldn't handle that.

After the Egypt rant, Dunphy went to Italy as he was obliged to do for the *Sunday Independent*. He walked into the press conference before the Netherlands match and Jack announced there'd be no comment unless Dunphy left, insisting that he wasn't a proper journalist and said it was up to the rest of the press to remove him. The Irish guys were determined that would be the case because they wanted the press briefing to go ahead, but the English journalists led by Ian Ridley who was working for the *Guardian* said no way, it was all in or all out. Dunphy was fascinated by the dynamic and really appreciated it.

Managers say they don't mind criticism as long as it's constructive, but the last thing they want is *any* kind of criticism. So Jack stormed off to his room, took the Irish lads with him and the English journos who championed Dunphy's cause got no copy. But Dunphy wouldn't budge in his views no matter how much the manager tried to bully him and how much the manager's words stoked the anger of the crowd. After that match against the Netherlands, Dunphy was coming out of the ground with Colm Tóibín, through a big coach park which involved a 100 yard walk and he maintains that "there were guys there just about ready to tear me apart". It was, he says even today, "quite savage."

It was worse for him back here. After we lost to Italy in the quarter-finals, Dunphy arrived on a flight about half an hour before the team landed, and the airport was packed. He got into a car with Greg Sparks, then an important advisor to Dick Spring and the Labour Party, and they drove to the roundabout. There were hundreds of thousands of people waiting for the team and when they saw it was Dunphy they moved on the car. There were no police, the car had to stop and Dunphy says it got very scary. They were thumping the windows, getting more and more aggressive and shaking it from side to side as if they were going to turn it over.

Dunphy told Sparks to get out and see if he could find a Garda and he legged it off down the road, leaving Dunphy on his own for about 10 minutes. Half of the crowd wanted to kill him and the other half were convincing people to leave him alone. At one stage two women came up and asked would he wind down the window for a photograph. Not wanting to antagonise anyone any further he thought he'd better comply at that stage so they took a photograph and then told him to "go fuck yourself". It was funny afterwards but not at the time because it was in the afternoon, there had been plenty of drink taken and this was a mob. A Garda finally came and said, "Eamon, don't go down the Drumcondra Road, go out by Portmarnock and around," and that's how he got home to Ballsbridge. To say he was pretty shaken by it all was one of the understatements of the millennium.

That is the trouble in being a panellist. If you are objective and forensic in judging a team and its players, not all the punters want that. But the reaction, horrendous though it was, showed how we had gone from being an irrelevance to a staple of television. Everyone tuned in and everyone had an opinion on us just as much as they had an opinion on whatever game was taking place.

The whole World Cup coverage was manic and myself and the two lads did it on our own in a little room in Studio 6, just down the hall from our current Studio 4. We were so busy we were eating on the run because we were covering all the matches, one after another, and going home knackered. One day blurred into another — bed, getting up and starting into it all over again. It was relentless and it was hard work. When Ireland went out of it, I brought the lads across the road to Elm Park Golf Club — the same place I'd sat with David Thornley and Ted Nealon years before — for food and they still remember that as a special occasion. After all the pressure, we were sitting in a diningroom with a table cloth, knives and forks, being served graciously. It's amazing how little things can become a treat but this was after three matches each day. We did it, though, and we got through it.

So did the country. Just. Even the Pope's visit didn't stir up the passions of the Irish like that particular fortnight. It was a very special time, there was a great sense of pride, a wonderful mood of national celebration, and it transformed soccer from being the least important of the national games to being possibly the most important, certainly for that month. The relationship with the team and people was very strong and the fact that the World Cup was being played in Europe too meant fans could come and go to the Ireland games. It was a bonanza for the airlines and the tour operators. Granted, Con Houlihan famously wrote that he missed that World Cup because he was in Italy and from the point of television, it was in the right timeframe for people to watch in primetime and celebrate it right here. When it was over, Gerry Ryan, God rest him, had me on the radio and asked if I regretted not being in Italy. "Not at all," I said, "Dublin was a very special place during Ireland's World Cup and I would not have missed it for the world." I knew exactly what Houlihan meant.

As a panel, we celebrated too and people tend to forget that after all the criticism of our comments. Calls were made to the station demanding to take us off the air because we were "unpatriotic". We faced criticism when we were out and about, but people didn't see our reaction to the penalty shoot-out win over Romania. As the nation held its breath, to quote George Hamilton's immortal words, we were cheering like fans and dancing around the studio. I was always sorry our coverage didn't come back to us in studio a little earlier and show our celebrations. So much for being considered po-faced, we were like all Irish fans enjoying every minute.

But when it finally did cut back to the studio I had a ridiculous hat on. The floor manager was Tadhg De Brun, his son was there watching and he gave it to me before the cameras came back on. It had two hands that clapped on the front of it, that part was broken, but I put it on anyway. When I look back at that clip, it's clear to me that we wanted the Irish to do well like everyone but broadcasting has a different imperative and on air we have to put our emotions to one side for the most part. If we didn't, people would have said these guys are not worth listening to.

Besides, the night of the Italy game, the three of us were in step with the national mood. The build-up was enormous and we felt we were a part of something huge. Realistically, we were not favourites and there was a sense that we had got as far as we were going to and a certain fatalism was accompanied by depression as well. As bad as Ireland were at times, and as good as they might have been, we didn't want it to come to an end.

According to the most comprehensive audience research conducted on behalf of RTÉ which included pubs, hotels, as well as homes, the penalty shoot-out in Genoa attracted the biggest ever audience for an RTÉ programme. I was told that some 90 per cent of the population over the age of four years watched the programme. It was phenomenal and Italia '90 established our panel as a powerful force in soccer comment. We had comprehensively bigger audience figures than BBC or ITV and reaction to the comments of Giles and Dunphy became national talking points. Ireland matches were not always entertaining but audience research showed programmes peaked when the panel discussed a game. Giles was hugely popular because of his sober reflective comment, and, even if Dunphy was public enemy number one, to some his passion made the headlines and grew the audience. My role? I was the facilitator, not an analyst, but the lads say my questioning brought the best from them.

There was an inevitable anti-climax once the World Cup was over but we were in the process of building trust with the people so everything we did was exciting. Even after it ended, we were in the midst of doing something very special. That continued on into the next World Cup but by USA '94 Dunphy wasn't here again and the show was the worse for it, especially after what that team went through to get there.

My brother Jack was at the final qualifier against Northern Ireland in Windsor Park with a couple of his kids and he told me he was never in a situation so toxic. He felt it was so dangerous that none of them got up to celebrate Alan McLoughlin's goal. In fact, they didn't start shouting and cheering until they got back to their car and that was predominately the case with away fans that night. By any measurement it was an appalling situation not helped by Billy Bingham who proved, in the opinion of many, that he didn't have any real sense of all-Ireland solidarity. He was right at home too as Windsor Park is primarily a sectarian enclave and the IFA have never faced up to that fact. As long as it's their home ground they won't get the next generation of James McCleans to play for them, something they have turned a blind eye to when they should have faced it years ago in the name of progress.

But back here Dunphy saw no progress either. Right through the Charlton years, he was busy challenging conventional wisdom but then walked out on the show ahead of the 1994 World Cup. Nell McCafferty, Nuala O'Faolain and others were brought in by Tim O'Connor who wanted different strands of society represented. When Dunphy heard that his exact words were, "If that happens, you can f**k off and I'm going to America."

Dunphy had quite a narrow view of that. The plan was that the panel would have its say and these people from outside the game would be brought in at the end for their views as part of the inclusive national event. Once they gave their take the panel would respond to it. It was a different concept but no matter how much we gained by inclusiveness, we lost more because it drove Dunphy away. Granted, it didn't drive away many viewers and the Norway game in '94 — which was appalling — was the biggest audience of all time in Ireland at 1.7m.

After all that, these days UK journalists are very aware of what we do. In the old days we used to go from Lansdowne Road to the Berkeley Court after and they would say, "Why can't we have the same in the UK". The *Guardian* has reported very favourably on us and saying this is the comment they should get in Britain, the *Telegraph* recently had a piece which was very complimentary too and we are considered in UK media eyes far ahead of what they have in England. But there was never an attempt to poach the lads and this is partly explained by money. The investment in the British game is huge and it would not be in their interests to have analysts constantly rubbishing the product. If you have someone saying a team is rubbish every time they play, people will eventually turn off and then the multi-billion pound project is in trouble.

Over here though, we have the freedom to say what we want. And as talk moves away from Brady's sunburn and the lads tune into the game, I know from their remarks watching on that they will say what they believe and it won't please everybody.

****

Towards the end of our meeting earlier, it was time to do some actual work. Brady had finished his fry quite quickly and expected everyone else to move on because he was ready. "Eugene is still eating. He rollicks us out of it if we're late and tells us to be here at 6pm, now we're waiting for you to finish your food. Come on will you," he said.

Eugene didn't budge and waited until he was good and ready before engaging. "So let's quickly go through the rest of the programme then and make sure you guys are happy with the inserts we propose to use. So we are going to have a longer
chat-time post-match. If it goes to extra-time we have to take an extra break and we are off the air half an hour later. Half-time is about four minutes. John you might see something and take over there. We have highlights later of the other game, Eamon, do you want to talk about that?

Dunphy nodded.

"We'll probably touch on financial fair play. There should be some information there. You each have information on pen pics, money spent, press kits for tonight's matches and that should be it. Now let's go and have a look at these pieces and make sure we are happy with them."

We stood and headed around the corner to a tiny suite

where there's a computer with the clips that had been picked out by Giles and he talked the lads through some of them. One he emphasised. "That one, particularly, but look at the build-up in the other one. Good players don't do that. But even if he doesn't start, keep that clip to show the difference in relation to that position. Not great shots but at least he is threatening. OK, lads? Is that too long for you, Eugene? It's a minute long."

"It's our opening piece so if you need all that then take it," was the reply.

"You are the chief, the senior analyst and the Grand Marshal, you deserve a minute," smiled Dunphy at the back.

"Well you can drop one of them if you can and show the passing in one of them for a little bit longer if you want," said Giles, ignoring Dunphy. "Alright, that should be that," he added.

They got up to come here to studio but Eugene called them back as there was one more clip to go through and he settled a bet between Dunphy and Brady over the nationality of the strikers before going in search of the teams. "Right, check BBC, Twitter, club websites for any sign of them and can you get some printed information on financial fair play too," he told those behind the scenes.

We head for studio and Dunphy picked up his homemade curry which was sitting in a plastic bag. "You shouldn't be eating from the canteen; you should be bringing in your food from home. Is that chicken you have, Eugene? Where do you think that chicken came from? It probably came from Thailand."

"All the way," said Brady, joining in.

"You wouldn't like that, Liam, you'd want a big greasy rasher on top of a load of chips covered in saturated fat."

No one can escape Dunphy when he's in that form. He

even passed a member of the 'Prime Time' team. "No controversy in here," he was laughing. "None at all, we don't do that in sport. We do Grand Marshals though. And what a Grand Marshal we have, come over here John."

Finally Eugene dragged him away. "Right lads, a respected journalist has tweeted this and here is the home team. Come on, it's 10 to seven, everyone should be heading to studio about sevenish. So the usual, Studio 4."

We've been here ever since but, hopefully, if we get a goal in the closing stages of the game, we won't be here all night.

CHAPTER 7

Anchorman

We finally get a goal so we won't be here all night. I know this because I can hear the roars echoing down the corridor from the studio. It's just my luck that I popped out for a second and missed the highlight of the game. In fact before I heard the reaction from the lads, I was just thinking of how uneventful the night has been and how that's not always a bad thing. After all, the most eventful time I've ever had in studio was one I wish I could forget as, on February 15, 1995 the infamous Lansdowne Road riots took place while we were on air and they were among the most worrying moments of my life.

My daughters Jill and Sally love sport of all kinds and around that time Sally went to all the big soccer matches she could get to. She was in her early teens and I got her and two friends Dara and Darina tickets for that game with England and because of the hype surrounding it she was more than excited when I left home to come to RTÉ for the evening. As always, I told her to enjoy it, be careful and I'd see her later.

Because the Irish supporters had been so wonderful I never saw a problem about her going to games without an adult. Even when Irish fans go away they policed themselves. They'd go abroad, have a few drinks, sing and enjoy the occasion but it stopped there. There was never any trouble because they took their reputation as good sportspeople very seriously. No Irish fans were allowed sully that well-earned reputation and for home games it was safer still. I knew myself from working at internationals in Dublin that they were events to be enjoyed rather than venues to go to with some sort of violent agenda. It had even gotten to the stage where the English media would openly admit that when Ireland didn't qualify for major tournaments, there was a void in the atmosphere. That night was no different and the Irish fans wanted again to show the world our good side.

There was no suggestion that night that it was going to be tense. England come to Dublin so rarely there was, in fact, a great sense of anticipation and everyone was looking forward to the game because it was in the midst of a great era of Irish soccer and England were the gold standard because of the interest here in their club football. Nobody, for one minute, anticipated any trouble. Not the Gardaí, the FAI, the media or the public in general. That, of course, was part of the problem which developed when you reflect on placing the English fans within the ground on an upper tier and the reaction time of the riot squad once trouble broke out.

There would have been a consciousness that certain elements of the English support were very dangerous, the world knew that. But no one thought this could happen in Dublin and perhaps we were naive because of the Irish tradition that you go to sport for sport. Giles told me afterwards that when he began his football career in England and first played for Manchester United, both sets of supporters mixed together and people went to games for the enjoyment of it all, like we here still do. But when people who are English-based, like Souness for instance, came here to work with us, he'd look at Croke Park and was astonished at the mixing of fans without trouble. It's changed dramatically in England to the extent that the philosophy of sport is different. Sadly, our innocence and our sense that sport is to be enjoyed for its entertainment did us no favours that night and the result was the most dramatic television for a long, long time.

I, too, was naïve, as I'd given Sally her tickets without checking on where she was sitting but when the trouble started, I was seriously afraid she would be caught up in it, yet it was my function to look at the disgraceful events as objectively as I could as an anchor. Not for the first time, my current affairs background came into play — I'm not saying for a moment that someone else couldn't have covered the story and anchored that show, but my media upbringing meant I was very comfortable during a breaking story like that. But, first and foremost, I was a father seriously worried about his daughter. I was so concerned that I actually said on air that my daughter was at the match, that I didn't know where she was but if anybody knew her and saw her, maybe they could look after her and get her out of there as quickly as possible.

In studio we began to realise that something wasn't right when the Nazi salutes started during the national anthems and the English fans began chanting "Ulster is British" and "Sieg Heil". It was like a scene from my days covering the Troubles up north for '7 Days'. Then David Kelly scored and there wasn't time to celebrate. Seats were ripped up in the Upper West Stand and thrown down on the Irish fans beneath. For all I knew Sally and her friends might have been directly in the area of the trouble and, while 20 were injured and thankfully no one was killed, I was thinking if a girl Sally's size was hit by a wooden bench coming from above, something tragic could occur. I have never been so afraid, I cannot emphasise that enough, and having to carry on and present the programme that was suddenly attracting an audience far greater than just sports fans made it a hard job. I had to keep my emotions under control and remain professional, hard as that was.

It was frightening in an immediate sense for more than me. There was great concern and worry about cameramen and staff who were working in the midst of it. Afterwards it emerged that one of our cameraman was placed right in front of the trouble and was stuck there, getting his pictures, yet trying to keep his head down. As it progressed, in studio we wondered if it could be contained, would it get out of control, who was likely to be injured and what would be the level of those injuries. Obviously within RTÉ there were two considerations — that no one covering the riot would be hurt and that those working at the ground would be able to continue to cover what was now a major international story and cover it well. That was a difficult balance but one I like to think we achieved.

From a studio perspective we stayed on the pictures from Lansdowne Road and everything we did from studio was voiceover. It worked out well because Giles and Dunphy were then so comfortable on television at that stage that they knew how to handle the change in the direction of the show. On top of that there were interviews over the phone from studio — the Minister for Sport Bernard Allen from Cork was contacted and Bertie Ahern used the occasion to lay the blame on English thugs in no uncertain terms. But the real hard work was done at the stadium and we were the Greek chorus in the background, not the focus. Instead all eyes were on Lansdowne Road where Jack Charlton was becoming more and more angry. He might be seen as an honorary Irishman with a great affection towards us but we had learned during Italia '90 he was deeply English and very conscious of his background and his people. He was ashamed of what they were doing.

We spoke to spectators on air who gave us eye witness accounts on what was now an emergency. It was the most dramatic sports night in Dublin in our television lifetime but it had little to do with sport. It was about unrest, about English fans out of control, about anarchists and thugs bred in a deteriorating English social climate that Giles had so often talked to us about in studio over the years.

As I watched events unfolding I had to maintain professional objectivity. But all the time in my head, I could hear myself saying "Is Sally OK? Is Sally OK?" Had I known she was in the East Stand, I'd have been fine. But at the ground, thankfully, was Andrew Kelly who used to work in my PR company, was once a correspondent in RTÉ and is now director of corporate affairs in Aer Arann. He recognised Sally, looked after her and her friends and brought them back to this very studio. We were barely off the air when he arrived with her and her friend and you can imagine my relief and how grateful I was. I think Sally was a bit annoyed that she was bundled up and brought home, though, because at that age, she was almost enjoying the drama and did not fully understand the danger. She was in the middle of something historic but as a Dad that wasn't my view of things.

So quiet nights aren't always the worst but as I jog back into studio to catch the replay of the goal, the panel are anything but quiet. After all these years they are still so passionate and while I'm relieved there'll be no extra-time and that we'll be getting out of here sooner rather than later and I'll get a good night's sleep ahead of another day in the office tomorrow, the rest of them are reacting for a very different reason. They are still entranced by the game, by good football and by goals.

"Look at the flick, John, look at the flick," says Dunphy in a tone of voice that's bubbling over with excitement. "Did you see it, Liam? Look," he says again. Brady is just as excited. Giles can appreciate the skill but is down to earth as always. "Make sure you get that replay to start off the clips afterwards," says Giles to Ciarán, our floor manager, before engaging with the lads. "I told you it was coming," he says and for emphasis repeats himself. "I told you it was coming."

****

Giles, Brady and Dunphy are the reason I enjoy our soccer coverage so much. I'd go so far as to say that I find nights like this relaxing because the guys are easy to work with and we understand our particular roles. They understand that my function is to bring out the main points of the game and so make them look good. I don't try and minimise what they are saying but they also recognise I have to represent the audience, I ask tough questions when appropriate and I have to challenge them too on behalf of the audience.

That's not to say I don't enjoy the other roles I have as an anchor away from football and I've always had an affinity with the Olympics. But that's a very different and sometimes more detached experience for the audience. People tend not to understand the many sports as they only surface on TV once every four years. Everyone knows the form players and the form teams in soccer, but viewing many Olympic sports is more about curiosity, blind hope and sometimes complete ignorance. Because of that, the interviews we conduct with the experts in studio aren't always about the intricacies of an event, rather about explaining the basics of that event before getting anywhere near those intricacies.

The lads might slag me off but they've all commented from time to time about the volume of literature I'll read in advance of a game and the amount of cuttings I arrive with, just in case they become relevant in the course of a conversation. At home people see the tip of the iceberg but, underneath the waterline, there is so much work and study. So you can imagine what an Olympics is like because so often it's not a question of topping up my knowledge but starting from scratch. They are not events we live and breathe and while it may seem like I'm as comfortable talking about the modern pentathlon as a Champions League match, that's down to a vast amount of research in advance. But then there's another problem. If tonight my role, as I see it, is to ask the questions a punter would, what would a punter ask of showjumping or swimming or shot putting? It just doesn't seem as natural an experience.

For that reason, it can be hard to get as excited by what you don't fully understand but that isn't to say there haven't been Olympic moments where we were thrilled and stunned and shocked. When you've covered as many Olympics as I have — London was my 10th having started in 1972 and missing out Los Angeles with that heart attack — of course there's been plenty of drama, both good and bad. In fact my very first Olympics in Munich brought about the most drama of any Games, for all the wrong and most horrifying reasons. But there was drama in other years too, and, from my perspective, not all of it was grounded in reality.

I was caught out by Mike Murphy for his candid camera programme during the Moscow Games but I didn't allow him use the footage. In the run up to a big, live programme like that, I'd normally be in studio 30 minutes before we go on air to make sure all systems are good to go and I can get comfortable. That programme was starting around 12 noon

but I arrived into the studio with less than 10 minutes to air, which was very unusual for me. I had a meeting which delayed me and I had no choice but Tadhg De Brún was the floor manager and he seemed
seriously concerned and wondered where I had been.

"I was at a meeting, it just finished and I came straight here as fast as I could," I said.

"Look at the time, do you know there's been an objection to the silver medals won by the Irish sailors," he retorted.

I was surprised to say the least because we'd all enjoyed David Wilkins and James Wilkinson's performance and presumed everything was as it seemed. But I barely had time to ask what had happened as a clearly flustered Tadhg said the editor wanted to do a recorded interview on it. "I know nothing about sailing," I warned him, but he was having none of it. "Listen, you are long enough in the business to do an interview about anything for two minutes. We've got a window here from the BBC and there are some notes on your desk direct from the event in Tallinn and they'll fill you in on the story. Read them quickly as the interview is ready to go." I went through the information which said there was an objection from one of the French delegation to the Irish silver medal due to a technicality. And it was Monsieur Le Febre, a French delegate, that was on the line ready to be interviewed.

I asked him a whole series of questions and got the most convoluted answers. At the conclusion I turned to the audience and said I didn't have a clue what he was talking about and I'd let them make up their own minds about it. Then I heard, "Well, O'Herlihy, it's obvious you know shag all about sailing". It was Murphy all along. Initially, I had no problem with it but afterwards reconsidered. If it had been done outside my working environment, no problem, but this was different. "With all due respect, I don't want you to make a fool of me doing my job," I told him. Maybe I was being pompous but others agreed and said I shouldn't under any circumstances let it be seen by the wider world. It's one thing to be the butt of a joke in a normal situation, but if someone is laughing at your work, then it undermines your authority.

The piece was very amusing but frankly a little destabilising. Every time someone came to studio to be interviewed that day I was wondering if it was again Mike Murphy dressed up. He was, in my view, the world's greatest candid camera presenter with a fantastic ability to perform in a huge variety of situations. Fred Cogley told me once that he sat in make-up and talked with Mike and didn't even recognise him. But having caught me out, Mike was very disappointed and a bit cranky about my reaction. In the end, he understood, even if he didn't necessarily approve.

I stuck to my theory on having a sense of humour away from work when I was caught out in the taxi on 'Naked Camera'. My daughter Jill, who now runs the company, set that up on the night I won the Television Personality of the Year Award. When my car was in for servicing, it was considered the perfect opportunity to catch me and since my PR company has a taxi account, when I got called to go get my car and jumped into the cab, I had no idea who the driver was; I just thought he was a right eejit. Even when I got out of the taxi, I still didn't know I had been set up. I began telling people, "Do you know I've been driven out here by the biggest eejit I ever met. I'm certainly going to get on to the company and complain about the quality of the drivers". Then the cameras came after me and I was caught round as a hoop! PJ Gallagher said later one of his great achievements was to be the first person to get Bill O'Herlihy to swear on air.

Then there's 'Aprés Match'. I love it, so do the lads but Giles
has the reservation that lampooning those who make the
show is not a good thing. He most often does not watch it.
Are 'Aprés Match' character sketches accurate? Yes, say my
panellists, and override any consideration that I don't say
"okey doke", "loive" or speak in a broad Cork accent. But I
have no doubt 'Aprés Match's' work has increased our pro-
files in a way that's been good for us. I remember speaking
to Colm Murray, sadly now the victim of motor neurone
disease, who was concerned at the impact a sketch on him
might have on his credibility. He was considering a protest
and future ban. "Don't dream of it," I said. "What they are
doing will lift you out of the run of newsroom journalists
and give you a special cache." He dropped any protest he
intended and told me later I was correct.

Besides, soccer has been a doddle through the years in
comparison to the Olympic Games which because of the
range of sports is tough work. Hours of research is needed to
prepare for programmes and make sure the interviews with
sports specialists make sense and add to the understanding of
a particular discipline.

London went well for us and for the team and our boxers
did us proud. But it was a relief the Games went without a
hitch from an Irish perspective with none of the equestrian
drugs drama we had in Athens and Beijing or none of the
controversy of Atlanta. What happened in Athens in 2004
and Beijing when doping allegations centred on some of our
horses shamed Ireland. From my point of view as Olympic
anchor I was determined not to pull any punches in establishing why Denis Lynch pulled out of the Beijing final. I had
a terrific editor in Colm Magee whose background had been
in current affairs and he, like me, was determined to get at
the truth.

We were not experts in areas equestrian so he made contact with those who knew the sport. If drugs are involved, he was told by a heavyweight figure in the sport, it could not have happened by accident. The information we got gave us the foundation for a strong, informative interview in the public interest. I did a tough piece with Avril Doyle, the former Fine Gael Minister who was head of the Equestrian Federation, backed up by Marty Morrissey who did a fine probing piece with Dermot Heneghan, Ireland's Chef de Mission for the Beijing Games.

During all that, not for the first time, I wondered about the role of the Olympic Council of Ireland. Their view that policing the sport was a matter for the Equestrian Federation struck me as the Pontius Pilate syndrome, of washing their hands of the problem. Not good enough, I thought then, and I think the same today. It's not as if the OCI are over burdened by developing sport in Ireland — they have little enough to do and ensuring all those at the Olympics are clean should be a priority.

But those equestrian incidents were mere footnotes when you think of the storm of controversy that surrounded Michelle Smith back in 1996. Of course there was and is no proof of any wrongdoing but just from the perspective of trying to stay on top of the achievements and rumours and accusations, it was manic. Despite all the broadcasts I've done and events I've covered across current affairs and sport, anchoring the Atlanta Olympics was a time of extraordinary drama, innuendo and opinion.

There were many in swimming who thought that something wasn't right and that something big and controversial was about to creep over the horizon. After all, Smith had gone from 90th in the world to first in just a three-year period. On top of that her coach, and eventual husband, was the

Dutch discus thrower and shot putter Erik de Bruin, who was in the midst of serving a ban for drugs. There seemed too many coincidences. Taking drugs is not about competition, it's about training so those who cheat usually don't have anything in their system come competition but Michelle was adamant that her improvement and success came about because of a new training regime and had nothing to do with cheating.

We had a big meeting before those Olympics that involved bringing all the specialists together like John Treacy, Eamonn Coghlan and Mick Dowling who would be commenting on the various sports of greatest interest to the Irish. I asked the question then and there regarding our approach to Michelle Smith but most of those in attendance didn't understand what I was getting at and the general reaction was, "What do you mean?" It was my opinion that something wasn't right and I said, speaking without any evidence, "We were very smart when it came to our handling of drugs and the sprinters in Seoul, so what will we do about Michelle?" There was an even greater silence and yet more puzzlement.

There was, they said, no evidence to support any suggestion of cheating. They were right, there wasn't but there were many in swimming who felt uneasy that Smith could not have been performing at that level naturally. "OK," I told the room. "Let's see what the scale of the issue will be." I turned to Gary O'Toole who was our swimming analyst.

"Gary, how big an issue will we face?"

His answer was a measure of his knowledge and of the issue.

"For certain, she is going to win two gold medals," he replied, "my judgment is she is going to win three gold medals and there is a distinct possibility she will win four."

The room was stunned. "There you are," I said. "Now what

do we do? What will be our editorial position?" But the truth was, despite any misgivings, there was no evidence against her. But we came in for huge criticism from certain quarters because of our silence on the issue.

There was a great sense of national occasion when she won those medals, just as O'Toole had predicted, and it reminded me a lot of the 1990 World Cup. In her first final, she was favourite and as we watched in studio there was the strangest atmosphere. On the floor there is what's called a lazy mic which conveys our conversation to the gallery and as they listened to Gary and I talking in studio in the hours before the race, there was concern about what we might say on air. We had to be very careful. Niall Cogley was the Olympics editor, and into my earpiece he said in a worried but decisive tone, "Bill, you don't say anything now until I clear all this because there are all sorts of libel connotations". By chance, the Director General Joe Barry was meeting with the Head of News in the Television Centre that day so we weren't long in getting a response. The message came down the line to us: "Unless there was hard evidence, you will say nothing and you will not spoil the mood of national celebration".

That was that.

From my perspective as a journalist, that was tough to take because my strong opinions and those of Gary were silenced. But, editorially, it was, of course, the right decision. Conjecture is not evidence and there was, and is, no evidence. Not everyone understood. Tom Humphries, and, yes, even Dunphy, in their newspaper columns gave us stick for not having the courage to stand up for what we believed. There was no evidence whatsoever to suggest drugs were involved so RTÉ would not tolerate any such comment or implication. It was tougher for Gary as I believe he felr that he was forced on national television to talk about her triumphs without alluding to what he perceived to be a serious issue.

Frustrating it might have been but on the other hand, it would have been outrageous to make any claim without evidence. The editorial call was legally correct if, in my mind, difficult to take. Not surprisingly, Gary and I were muted in our celebration of the golds in comparison to what might have been but as Smith continued to succeed, it was something which could not be ignored.

Finally, Niall Cogley came up with a half-way solution by showing in full a 20-minute press conference with Janet Evans of the USA in which she talked about the elephant in the room. It was the only way we could introduce the subject, far from ideal and small consolation given our personal views, but at least we didn't avoid it altogether.

I also had to talk to Michelle's family live during one broadcast and that was embarrassing. Hugely embarrassing. My heart wasn't in it after the Janet Evans interview but at the same time we couldn't show that to the audience. They were nice people who probably had no idea of what we were thinking, but I just felt that it was just so contrived and cheesy. I always found Michelle a very nice person and she made a brilliant impression in Atlanta when, you'll remember, President Clinton sought her out but that doesn't affect my perception.

Oddly enough, she once applied for a job with me and I found her to be hugely intelligent but I told her that I could not afford to employ someone who would be missing for so much time because of swimming. She never tried to hide her commitment to her sport and was honest and up front about it. Had she not been so busy with swimming, that job would have been hers because it was very obvious how talented and driven she was. In fact after the Olympics I met her at a reception. She was in great form and while I didn't mention my suspicions and my opinion, I did say to her, "What you should do is retire, you have three gold medals, cash in on that. Make as much money as you can and as many waves as possible out of the pool". She didn't listen to me though and her husband obviously had a different view. It was a huge mistake. She had nothing else to achieve but in time tested positive for Androstenedione. She was banned for four years which effectively ended her career. Worse still, given how vocal she was about her innocence after the 1996 Olympics, it inevitably cast further shadows that added to the doubts in the minds of people like me. After that, I never had the chance to confront her because she has never permitted herself to be in that situation. She avoided questioning and at one stage, pulled out of a 'Late, Late Show' appearance because she didn't receive a guarantee that her swimming past would be completely ignored. She has never since wanted to talk about it publicly.

Some, of course, won't have a bad word said about her. During the Games, Jim Sherwin, commentating, was hugely enthusiastic. I reckon if I was commentator, I would have had the same enthusiasm because from an Irish perspective she was the perfect winner. She spoke the language, had red hair, was a lovely and warm person and a good interviewee. She had everything going for her and it was so easy to be caught up in the spirit of the occasion if you were poolside and take a much more subjective and personal view. Jimmy Magee defends her to this day though and I just cannot agree, despite my vast respect for him. His argument is very simple — there is no proof and no one ever took the medals from her, she still has them, and her times weren't that good. There is truth in what Jimmy says but it's not the whole story and there's my problem. Cathal Dervan, another respected journalist, wrote her book without any reservations.

It's been a subject that for us has lingered long past the actual event. During the Beijing Games I was talking on air to
Eamonn Coghlan about gold medallists and mentioned that
Ireland's last time to get an athlete at the top of the podium
was Michael Carruth back in 1992. I thought no more of it
but during the subsequent ad break, Coghlan's phone rang
and it was Smith. She was furious and said that unless we
retracted and corrected my statement, she would sue RTÉ
for ignoring her achievement. Coghlan knew her very well,
and when he put the phone down, said "Bill we could be in
trouble here". I had to come up with a completely fabricated
reason that allowed him to talk about her three gold medals,
I gave her a bit of a plug and that was the end of it. We had
no other option as she might well have sued us as she is now
a very good lawyer as well as being a very intelligent lady.

Aside from the Smith debate, Gary O'Toole got the recognition he deserved as an analyst and an expert on swimming.
This might offend others but he was the best contributor
I've been involved with across all the Olympics I've worked
on, and by a long way too. He has beautiful English and an
amazing ability to bring the audience with him in
swimming. When he did those Atlanta Games, nobody had a
notion about the sport and yet people were talking authoritatively about splits, starts and pacing and all kinds of technicalities because they found it so easy to listen to him and
understand the sport.

He tells a great story about his impact. Halfway through
the swimming programme he was coming into RTÉ and a
bus pulled up beside him. The driver opened the small window on the bus. "You are Gary O'Toole, I've been watching
you on the
television, you are terrific, you know everything. Will you do

me a favour and tell me what's going to win the 3.30pm in Galway." Gary was genuinely brilliant in his judgement and he would say that if she is to win, she must do this, this and this and must be in this position and under this time. The whole country was enthralled.

He was so good and made such an impact that by the end of the summer of 1996, the thought crossed his mind, and others, that he should consider giving up medicine and becoming a full-time broadcaster. I dissuaded him. "Gary, you are out of your mind," I told him. "First of all what would you be doing? There's an Olympics every four years and between times swimming is practically never covered. You'll do programmes you've no interest in or that wouldn't stretch you like an Olympics would. And you'll give medicine up for all that? I think you are crazy and my advice to you as a friend is don't dream of taking a job in RTÉ or any other television station."

He did a series afterwards that wasn't a big success but whatever overtures were made to him, he made his decision and turned down television as a career. I was glad and with that the Olympics disappeared for another four years. It's a novelty to enjoy whereas here and now is always with us and even though tonight's game is nearly over, it's never far until the next instalment of what can be a soap opera.

****

The lads retake their seats after the goal and I stride through the darkness, past the cameras and retake my own seat having missed the goal. I think that if this show has been the making of such a decent chunk of my life, then it's been the making of theirs too. For instance, it's given Giles and Brady a vehicle to remain at the forefront of the national soccer consciousness long after they hung up their boots but it's probably been most important to Dunphy. It's not just because he's been here since the beginning but because he has changed how people look at the dynamics of a panel, and in doing so, made himself a national celebrity whom everyone knows. His comment now stretches beyond soccer and even if he's talking about politics or the economy, people listen to what he has to say. He is up to date on all those matters but crucially he has the common touch and is in touch with what the masses think. Those masses will be cutting back to us in a matter of moments as the final whistle is just seconds away. "Are you happy, Bill, back to you from the commentary and then ad break in two minutes?" says Eugene from the gallery. I am and tell the lads what's in store. "You'll lead in with the goal," I say to Giles. "Of course he will," says Dunphy. "Senior analyst and Grand Marshal, who else could do it?" And with that, the atmosphere in the room changes as the red light on top of camera two blinks on. "Thank you very much, George, I have to say that was exhausting to watch," I say to the audience at home and the lads beside me. "It was," says John, "but at least it was in the balance right up to the end and there were chances after the break."

Dunphy is having none of it though and starts looking at ramifications and beyond just the 90 minutes. "They may have won and the leadership restored some unity but what next? You have to look at the dynamic of that dressing room. It's not right. The players have taken over." It's always a bigger picture with Dunphy.

I may have told Gary O'Toole that television wasn't the way to go, but I sometimes wished Dunphy did more. Politics may or may not have been for him, but I still think to this day he deserved a better chance as a television talk show host. He was immensely successful on radio but people may well forget his attempts at such a role with TV3, but they made the big mistake of going head-to-head with 'The Late, Late Show.' When he told me he was taking it on, I told him straight out he was mad and didn't stand a chance. He was adamant, though, that he was going to take out Pat Kenny and beat him for audience. His stubbornness cost him, as it turned out.

"You haven't a chance and it's nothing to do with Pat Kenny," I told him. "There's a cachet about 'The Late, Late Show' that transcends whoever the presenter and producer is. Look at the figures. It is 700,000 week after week going up to over a million. You cannot beat it. It's embedded in the Irish psyche so don't do it. Do it on a Saturday." If he'd listened there may well have been no Ryan Tubridy and no Brendan O'Connor because away from soccer, there is no doubt Dunphy is talented and controversial and people like that mix and like watching him.

But he didn't listen to me and after that it wasn't going to work. Figures weren't good enough but I do think TV3 made a huge mistake taking him off the air. They needed to face up to the fact they couldn't beat 'The Late, Late Show' and should have moved him to a Saturday where I believe he would have been a success. But instead they threw away the makings of a very good programme. Dunphy was very disappointed. He now recognises that he made a mistake but at the time didn't realise the dynamics of the audience relationship to 'The Late, Late Show'. He thought it could be taken based on the quality of his show when it has nothing whatsoever to do with quality. 'The Late Late' simply is an institution. If it goes on for another 30 years, no matter who presents it and who is on it, it will still pull in 700,000 a night.

I think Dunphy saw himself as capable of mounting a programme that would have rediscovered some of the dynamism of 'The Late, Late Show' from the early days. It would be tough, interesting and issue-based. In his mind it would be quasi-current affairs but not entirely current affairs. And Dunphy has a curious view of journalism and television. He said to me once that he thinks anyone that comes out of a school of journalism or studies it in university is actually hurt by the experience. They might learn the technicalities but they lose touch with real life and that "old school professionalism" is missing.

While he knew much that would have made him a good chat show host, he got a couple of things very wrong. For starters he looked at 'The Late Late' as it used to be and as the show that was one of the greatest influences on current affairs in Ireland along with '7 Days'. But, since then, current affairs has rediscovered its edge and is doing a much greater volume of broadcasting than before. 'Prime Time' is comprehensive and on top of breaking news stories. That's a very different landscape to the past and 'The Late, Late Show' and its producers don't, in my opinion, have the same appetite for current affairs. There has been a loss, though, and even if one could not go so far as to say it has dumbed down, times have changed and its niche has changed since the Gay Byrne days.

In today's economic situation people don't just come to Dublin at the drop of a hat. It's not like London or New York, and getting top class guests is difficult and, crucially, expensive. I remember one amusing incident when Jim Callaghan was Home Secretary in Britain and he was in the make-up department, ahead of an appearance. Vincent Scally, who was essentially the maître d' of Current Affairs, looked after the guests and got them to sign clearance forms. Callaghan's form offered him 50 Irish pounds.

"There's a few quid involved but it's only a token for your

favourite charity, perhaps," said Vincent, but Callaghan
looked at it with disgust and said, "50 pounds?" He was
appalled and insulted by the figure. Vincent looked at it
quickly. "That must be a mistake," he said and added another
nought. Callaghan was satisfied.

That was many, many years ago. The figures will have
changed and the costs grown dramatically and people constantly underestimate this. This is true especially now of
sport and difficult days lie ahead in a tough economic climate. We cut to a break but we're only minutes away from
the big finale as we screen the final ads and move towards the
last part of the show.

CHAPTER 8

This Isn't The End

Down here on the floor, there's calm, but in the gallery this is the hardest part of the night as they draw together all the different strands, cut them to fit and complete the show. In my ear, I can hear Eugene and those around him weave it all together, working against the clock.

"Sending that through now, it's 98 seconds."

"Nice one."

"Okay let's get that clip ready. Thanks."

"What's that clip number?"

"So those interviews are both worth it? So pull up item 89. We'll need to caption check."

"Did you get which of them was first up? Okay Bill, he's first up. How are we doing for time, are we okay?"

"Three minutes left on commercial break."

"Is that other match edit in, it should be ready? Okay, so we have two-and-a-half minutes chat on last night? And this chat is seven minutes all in."

"Yeah but we are two minutes and 20 seconds over."

"Okay, we'll bring it down. How long are these pieces?"

It's a cacophony of craziness and to an outsider sounds like chaos. Yet each knows what they are doing, it's a marvellous skill and Eugene gets back with instructions before the final ad break comes to a close. "Bill, let's get straight into these pieces. Just remind the boys there is a piece on the end of the interview as well. We'll save the rest for a promo somewhere else."

With that the music starts up, the countdown commences and we are back on air one last time for tonight.

"Welcome back," I say. "Now gentlemen, in terms of where they are going, what about this point made in some newspapers?" I pull out some clippings I brought along earlier and question their views by quoting the views of others in the media.

"It's winning football," says Dunphy.

"And it could win them it all?"

"I never said that Bill," he replies.

"Sorry, I misunderstood you," I say, but the others are in quick as a flash and that's how volatile it can be. It kicks off a debate that briefly rages so strongly that if you just wandered in you'd think the lads weren't even friends. I'm used to it, though, and it's nothing compared to some of the experiences we've had over the years. Indeed, never has it been more awkward than when Giles and Dunphy fell out. When that happened, I was stuck in the middle. It was the most awkward position for the anchor and I was trying to do my own job, get them to do theirs as well, and work through the obvious tension and anger.

It happened more than once. And although the first time was an age ago, that doesn't mean it is easily forgotten. It erupted over Dunphy's book about Matt Busby called 'A Strange Kind of Glory'. It was 1992 when it hit the shelves and Giles reviewed it for the *Evening Herald* and said he didn't feel by the end of the book that he learned more about Matt Busby than he already knew. It had taken Dunphy months to research the book, months to compile it, months to write it and in fact he lived in Manchester for six months so he could do the best job possible. He still regards it as the best thing he has ever done and maintains that it was full of new insight and new takes on the Busby era. Reviews in other newspapers backed that up and Dunphy was fuming that Giles, of all people and who played for Busby, couldn't see as much.

"You just hate Busby and I don't think you even read it," he'd say to Giles afterwards. "If you did read it you'd know that it's damning enough of Busby in a certain way, but then again, you didn't read it, did you?" Giles thought it would be more of an expose, and it was, although quite nuanced. But it was the phrase "I didn't learn anything that I didn't know before" which drove Dunphy mad. He continued to say it was an indictment of two years of work from someone who hadn't taken the time to read it. And by someone whose opinion would have huge influence.

Giles told me privately at the time that he didn't like it but wanted to write the least damaging review he could. I made sure his view stayed with me at the time and went no further as the situation was already a mess. "I just felt that for someone to say what John said meant they obviously hadn't read it or understood it because there was loads of stuff he couldn't have known because I spent two years on the road digging out stuff," Dunphy said afterwards. "I read this and rang him up and called him a f*****g c**t."

What was worse was that Giles' review came out the same day as the launch and, worse still, Giles was supposed to launch the book. During that telephone conversation, Giles was cordially uninvited and Tony Cronin ended up launching it instead at very short notice. For a couple of months after that, it was a nightmare in studio. I love coming to work in RTÉ but around that time it was just a horrible situation. On air the lads would discuss a game but as soon as the camera went off they'd go quiet and would not speak to each other. Tim O'Connor, of course, made it very clear that if there was any sign that this row was affecting the product, then they were gone. He was very blunt about it and I passed on the message. It led to a false cordiality between them on air even if there was a complete silence off it.

Finally, after many months it began to thaw. The first step to normality was taken when they started talking about a game they were watching off air and it was fitting that soccer saw them make-up. Giles and Dunphy had always been great friends and it was good to see that friendship restored and endure to this day.

There was, however, a hiccup along the way. The subject of the row was, surprise surprise, Roy Keane and his Dunphy-penned autobiography in 2002. And it was more serious in some respects even if it didn't last as long. In the midst of the Saipan incident, Dunphy described Giles — and Brady for that matter — as an "uncle Tom" on 'Questions and Answers'. Giles took huge offence to that and thought it was a disgraceful comment, as did his family. The three lads were coming from very different places during all of that and Dunphy would maintain that it was cordial until Giles started taking the high moral ground about Keane and Alf Inge Haaland.

"This is you talking, a notorious hatchet man who was much, much worse than Roy Keane, you who were reckless, who was icy, who was an assassin," Dunphy told him. And then on 'The Last Word', Dunphy went further and brought up John Fitzpatrick, a Manchester United player who, he claimed, had his leg broken and career ended by Giles when at Leeds United. It was extremely personal.

'The Last Word' went and found Fitzpatrick, had him on the show and it turned out Dunphy was wrong. He'd actually broken his knee, he did play again and he took Giles' side regarding the incident. The press came after Dunphy at that point and that only made him angrier still but, thankfully, Giles didn't sue him for his remarks and it blew over. It was a hell of a storm before it passed but Giles knew what kind of a person Dunphy was and that helped. Dunphy gets animated but he doesn't hold a grudge and sees these things as debates as opposed to rows no matter how much vitriol there is.

Take the Rod Liddle example. After Roy Keane left Manchester United the debate again involved Saipan and it was my job as always to get the best out of the lads. Dunphy had already said, "I think Niall Quinn is a creep," and started to savage Brady for his views on Quinn, but rather than giving Dunphy carte blanche, I decided to offer a contradictory and alternative view. I hinted at Liddle's column from the *Sunday Times* and Dunphy took off.

"If you are going to quote a gutter journalist calling Roy Keane a thug, you can do it on your own. If you are going to use Niall Quinn, soccer's Mother Teresa, you can do that on your own as well. There's loads of tabloid journalists out there, I'm not going to listen to that kind of crap... Who wrote it? I'll tell you who wrote it, Rod Liddle."

He went on to say why Liddle had no personal credibility. After that, though, Dunphy went on 'Liveline' with Joe Duffy and it turned out Liddle was on the other line. He was caught cold but apologised and said he was out of order and the two of them actually get on quite well now. That just shows how heated Dunphy can become but he can cool just as quickly and those in the firing line must understand that.

"These things happen," he said of the Liddle remark afterwards and almost wore it like a badge of honour because it wasn't forced and because it made great television.

Dunphy hates the idea of going through the motions in this job. All of us on the panel do. In terms of input, we have an hour-long editorial meeting before each game and even if they tend to wander in different directions at times, they cover a huge level of work before a game. That doesn't happen elsewhere; indeed Dunphy has said at more than one meeting, "Imagine Alan Shearer doing this?" So when a row breaks out, the lads actually quite enjoy it.

Also, you have to remember those incidents have been few and far over the course of 26 years and we have a surprisingly good-natured show, yet full of vitality. That's no mean achievement when you are talking about strong-minded people on set together, with no shortage of conviction. When you have been doing it together for so long, you have to be wary of complacency and consensus can be a disease. Maybe the occasional row isn't the worst thing but away from the guys, the only serious row in all the years that wasn't of our own making was with Glenn Killane, who was a dynamic Head of Sport before he became Managing Director of Television. He felt there was too much talk in the 45-minute lead-up to a game and demanded it be more visual. That caused a huge problem and underlined a fundamental point of contention: who runs the show — the analysts on the floor or the production team?

It's the eternal battle between good production values and good content as you can have a top-notch panel but a programme ruined by production gimmickry. Pre-produced packages will look good but they can interrupt good conversation and so the chat never gets off the ground. But television is not radio and goals and action are hugely important to the production, but if not chosen carefully and with editorial emphasis can create conflict with people who want to analyse comprehensively and who believe it's the contribution of the analysts which gives the show its special appeal. Television people argue that 45 minutes of talking with few visuals turns television into radio, which is unacceptable, so there was a high level of tension. When Killane put this forward during the 2006 World Cup, the analysts rose to the debate.

Graeme Souness was in the middle of it and said, "This is not my row," at which point he walked out. But he must have become bored because outside he found a hurley and a helmet, put them on, came back in and told us all he was well equipped for any row. Souness' cameo broke the tension and discussion produced the compromise of reasonable visual coverage to complement vigorous discussion. Both sides were happy. The panel felt they were still driving the programme from the floor and the executives felt they had again assumed control.

****

Never was there more debate than around Saipan and during that time I had to be on my game like never before because emotions often ran so high. I actually was late to the party on that. I was in a taxi in Dublin and the driver turned and said, "Did you hear Keane is coming home. "What?" I said and didn't believe him at first but he told me it was all over the radio and turned it on. I was listening to this in the cab and I was stunned. We wouldn't have been there without him and all of a sudden he wouldn't be there. Surely someone could resolve the matter, I thought. I was very wrong.

If I missed out on the breaking news, Dunphy was probably among the first to hear it. He was working in Today FM when it came through and he got a call from Michael Kennedy who was Keane's solicitor and, more importantly, his confidant and advisor. Kennedy asked Dunphy if he'd have a word with Roy because he wanted Dunphy to persuade Roy to go back to the squad. Dunphy agreed, got Keane's mobile but didn't do quite what he said he would.

Dunphy said: "Michael has given me a call, but I'm not going to try and persuade you to leave Manchester and go back. Do what you think is right for yourself and your family. It's a long way back."

It was a long way back and I was told that Keane hadn't walked out, but in fact he had been asked to leave. He tried to make it back but Mick McCarthy wouldn't listen and decided to put his foot down.

For Brady the news broke at an academy manager's meeting he was attending for Arsenal. He'd noticed his phone was almost continuously buzzing in his pocket. On a break he took a look and discovered a lot of media people wanting to speak to him. He dodged responding for a while, gave it some thought and tried to get the facts about what had happened before he gave any opinion. When he finally spoke, it was his belief that McCarthy was right to jettison him from the squad because Keane was out of order and the situation was detrimental to the team in their preparation for the World Cup.

I disagreed. Keane didn't see any need for him to be called in to justify what he said in front of all the players unless it was a deliberate attempt to get him out, which Keane believed it was. I met Alex Ferguson some time afterwards and he said to me it was the worst example of management he had ever seen. He was baffled that McCarthy could send home his star player but, far worse, how he could allow a situation be created in which Keane would inevitably explode. Ferguson was hugely critical of McCarthy. "How could you put Keane in a position where you knew for certain he would explode and would have no alternative but to go?" he said to me.

I couldn't get over the way it exercised Irish supporters, who were completely split down the middle. There were those who said you take your blows, play the World Cup and then do what you have to do afterwards. That would have been precisely Brady's take. "You get your head down, you make the best of it and resolve those situations another time," he said.

What was most striking, though, was that there was no neutral view, instead extremes on both sides and it looked to me as if the stance of fans depended on where they came from geographically. I supported Keane tribally but could see his point as well. Many in the squad forgot not just his importance on the pitch in getting the team there, but what he had done for them all off the pitch. He was the person who got the seating arrangement on planes changed at a time when the suits were up the front and he would have seen himself as an ambassador for the players. But he was temperamental, not always in good humour and that seemingly caused problems.

Saipan had a subtext too, background whispers, although I obviously could never verify them. Keane, it was said, was resentful of Niall Quinn and, more specifically, his testimonial. Gary Kelly's sister had sadly passed away with cancer and he had planned to donate the money from his testimonial to help build a cancer hospice in Drogheda and support another in Leeds. Everyone on the Irish team knew Kelly's plans and supported them. But then Quinn announced his testimonial and upstaged Kelly with the same type of plan in

Sunderland and Dublin. From what I heard, Keane resented Kelly being upstaged and would not go to the Quinn testimonial at the Stadium of Light, a game between Sunderland and Ireland, just days before they headed off for the Far East.

True or not, this was the last thing needed to stabilise the environment in Saipan. Denis Irwin said to me that anyone who calls Keane a party-pooper doesn't know him at all. He maintains he is the nicest guy you could meet and is seriously good fun. But he wasn't considered great fun in Saipan because he was on an island perceived as a stopover in trafficking of women from Asia to Europe for prostitution, he saw a team unprepared, a week away from the World Cup with no gear, no pitch, no goalposts, no footballs and they weren't the least bit bothered. Instead they were happy to go drinking with the media. That was not Keane's idea of preparation — remember his mantra: fail to prepare, prepare to fail.

Retrospectively, perhaps Keane should have been told, "Stay at home, come out a week later" and then he'd have been fine. He wasn't in the business of socialising with the media or practicing on a pitch he considered dangerous and on which you could break an ankle. The whole thing was a mess because of a chain of awful decisions, one after another.

Dunphy was central to the debate because he had just finished a book on Keane, which was yet to be published, and his connections meant he had a monopoly on the big interviews for his Last Word programme. Dunphy gave all sides an airing but he did have his own very subjective view and made no effort to conceal it. But everyone got to have their say and, given all this was happening before the World Cup, he was the one who got the rest of us involved. When I was on his radio show, I came out very strongly in support of Keane and Dunphy was delighted as a passionate supporter of Keane. It was a most extraordinary time and it produced this extraordinary incident.

Dunphy was on the air and when his programme went to an ad break he noticed his phone buzzing. He wouldn't normally answer but saw that the number was that of Keane. "There is a guy outside my gate, and he wants to interview me, he says his name is Tommie Gorman," said Keane. "What should I do?" Dunphy thought about it quickly and said, "People are going crazy here Roy, in your own interests you should give him an interview because he is a good journalist and he is sound. It will give you the opportunity to explain directly to the Irish people in your own words exactly why you have done what you have done. I think it's always better to come out and talk and that's my honest advice." With those words ringing in his ears, Keane let Tommie in. He thought the interview was a disaster. Afterwards Dunphy got another call. "What the f**k was all that about?" Keane asked. That may have been the beginning of the end of Dunphy's relationship with Keane.

As a broadcaster, the controversy hugely excited me but in an immediate sense I had no editorial role. We hadn't begun our coverage of the World Cup at that stage and the way RTÉ operates, any special programme would have been handled by the news or sports staff. My contractual obligation was the World Cup football coverage and so there was never any question of my being brought in to anchor a special programme. But I was itching to get in and kick-off our many debates which would be central to the action.

Finally our programme got underway and most of the discussion time was taken up with the Saipan controversy. At half-time in games, it was all that was talked about and when we cut back to coverage of other games, the Ireland situation still held centre stage. We were in studio when Niall Quinn did a major interview and spoke about how appalling the situation was. But he got no sympathy from the panel. Their attitude was he was talking out of both sides of his mouth and the stance he took in the interview should have been taken at the meeting between Roy, the management and the team. The lads were pretty sure he didn't. The row did immense damage to Mick McCarthy as well, because right or wrong and that's your personal judgment, he was destabilised as a consequence. I thought he was a good manager, our panel thought he was a decent manager as well, but this changed everything.

There were times on air when Dunphy thought I was coming out in support of McCarthy against Keane but that was based on me putting my views aside and instigating debate. Dunphy had always been a fan of Keane's and had been promoting him as one of the greats right through his career and also as one of the great motivators and captains. Thus, he was particularly strident in his support but he was also blind to the alternative view and couldn't take on board anyone else's opinion on the matter. It was all down to McCarthy and the FAI in his view and it annoyed Brady that Dunphy never saw the other side of the argument. Dunphy thought the lads were ganging up on him and he felt let down by Giles and me because we weren't backing up his point.

Little wonder, then, that off-air it was a seriously frosty World Cup. "We have fun on this show," Brady said to him. "But now and again something crops up and if you don't agree with us, then you call us all sorts of names."

Maybe it all took its toll on Dunphy, because there was an incident early on in that World Cup where he showed up the worse for wear. He told the *Irish Times* since: "Was I drunk? Of course I was drunk! Wouldn't you get drunk if you were on with Gerry Armstrong and Peter Collins at eight o'clock in the morning watching Russia and Japan? I thought it was pretty good grounds for having a few jars. Ray Houghton got me into that, kept me in Lillies until four o'clock in the morning. Ray wasn't working until the evening game. Ah, that was a dereliction of duty. I felt bad about that. But they didn't suspend me, they just sent me home for a few days."

Let's be clear about this. Dunphy wasn't thrown off the panel. It was suggested to him that it wasn't the best day for him to be on air and he was persuaded not to go on. Dunphy was reluctant but finally saw the wisdom of the decision. I know for a fact that it was handled very sensitively by Ryle Nugent, who didn't make a song and dance of the incident. If news travelled through the corridors of RTÉ it wasn't Ryle's doing. He was protecting Dunphy, even if Dunphy perhaps did not see it like that at the time. Ryle handled it quietly, explained afterwards why he did it and once it was over, that was it. Dunphy was back on the air very quickly.

I wasn't on air at the time and when I heard about it, I took the view that something like that wouldn't have happened unless Ryle had a very justifiable reason for taking the decision he did. Dunphy is a valuable commodity to RTÉ and it would not have served Dunphy's or RTÉ's purposes to have him on air when not appropriate. Dunphy might not always be the best judge of that and in this case he clearly wasn't. Ryle did it in the best interest of person and programme, he had no other agenda so I would have been 100 per cent with him.

Moments like that don't help but Dunphy has a reputation that is completely distorted. He loves a good time but he's not out on the town morning, noon and night as people seem to think he is. Despite his comment about not being able to get good cocaine in this town he leads a relatively quiet life but when he does go out, he really enjoys himself. But that was one time he shouldn't have.

Back at the World Cup, Ireland did reasonably well but that, in my mind, only reinforced Keane's point that this was a poor tournament yet we weren't focusing on the chance that we might win it. Keane thought we could have gone a long way and he couldn't understand why the Irish team were messing about on a Mickey Mouse island. We did well but with Keane we would have done a lot better.

It was a seismic World Cup for more than Keane, though, and its effects lingered on through other regimes. After a poor start to Euro 2004 qualifying, McCarthy lost his job but that grated with people and made things awkward for Brian Kerr. He didn't help himself either though and while I liked him, the lads thought he was arrogant. In terms of an Irish manager for the Irish job he was the choice of the Irish journalists because he was both popular and successful with underage teams. He became increasingly unpopular, however, as time went on. I met him at a function towards the end of his tenure and said, "Brian, you know I'm one of your fans but I think you are making a right balls of this".

"What do you mean?"

"Well you are becoming very dismissive of the Irish media, you're perceived to be unhelpful to the guys that helped put you in the job and they are the guys that will damage you if you don't play the game. Especially if results go against you."

"Well I'm sick and tired of being asked the same questions, day after day after day after day."

"Sure, I can understand that can get you down. But what you have to do is structure something, even once a week, and give everyone a week's supply of information."

Maybe he wasn't bothered or it wasn't possible but it didn't happen and that did Brian no favours. I thought he handled the media badly towards the end, but when you look at the latitude afforded to Trapattoni by the FAI he was in my view treated shabbily.

I don't understand why Trapattoni is still managing Ireland. Sure he qualified us for the Euros and brought us to the play-offs in the World Cup and nobody can deny him these achievements but our performances against Croatia, Spain and Italy were abysmal. Worse still, the game against Kazakhstan was, arguably, Ireland's worst performance for years even if we scraped a lucky win. I subscribe to the view Trap has nothing more to give and that he's caught in a football time warp while the game has moved on.

It astonishes me that someone paid over €1 million is not obliged to go to games and see what players are available to Ireland beyond those he calls up on a regular basis. Giles has told me time and again you cannot judge a player on a DVD, you must see him in action but Trapattoni makes a virtue of watching players on DVDs and then, it could be argued, rushing to judgement.

Is Trapattoni good for the Irish game? I don't think so. His game is stereotyped, defensive, tied to a system which can be exploited and unlikely to be replicated in the nation's lower leagues. He's surprisingly indiscreet in his comments about players and his treatment of Long, Gibson, McClean and Foley was so insensitive in public. The Irish soccer fans did not appreciate his comments nor his commitment to players clearly not of international standard. But Trapattoni is his own man and he'll point to near qualification in 2010 and qualification in 2012 as the major positives of his time in charge. He has his supporters but I believe there is, increasingly, a disconnect between the Irish team and its supporters. His system rules, players are chosen to suit the system regardless of the quality of others available to Ireland who are neglected game by game. I'm thinking of Coleman, Hoolahan, Pilkington, Ireland and Clark.

Not that Liam Brady would ever agree with my views. He knows Trapattoni well and says he always does things his own way, won't be swayed by anyone and if he fails, he fails but he's not the kind of man to listen to journalists or pundits when making his decisions. He has his own reasons for picking the players he does. Brady would have seen us on air the odd time during his role as assistant manager to the national team but said he didn't need to because he knew what we would be saying. "I'd be in your corner as well," he told me, "I like football to be played in an open style but that was a great experience for me to learn that Trapattoni had his way of getting results and no matter what was said to him, that was always the way he was going to cut his cloth. I'd like to watch Ireland play brilliantly and win but sometimes given the players, we have to go a different route to get our results and that was his thinking from the start."

Interestingly, Brady also said that during his two years in the dressing room, quite a few times players would mention Dunphy's name and quote his opinions to Trapattoni and the fact he thought they should be doing things a very different way. Trapattoni, seemingly, would just look at them and it was water off a duck's back. He had people on his case in Italy over the years; he'd heard it all before and couldn't have cared less.

One had to be sympathetic to Trap that night in Paris for the World Cup play-off though. So much went wrong, although when John O'Shea had to go off and Paul McShane came on, there was a huge groan in the studio and immediately came the view, "This is an accident waiting to happen." The lads regarded McShane as very game, had a lot of time for him as a person, but reckoned he is prone to a lapse of concentration that could lead to a major error. They unanimously felt he was the wrong person at the wrong time to

200

come into that match. He wouldn't have been their choice at all. They subscribed to the view that the handball goal was the fault of McShane, and Shay Given, as Thierry Henry should never have gotten a chance. The handball was outrageous and there were two guys offside, but they could have prevented it.

Was the French win and the handball part of a conspiracy against Ireland? FIFA would not have wanted a small nation like Ireland to go forward and the belief that a conspiracy existed against Ireland was fuelled by allowing the goal. It was ironic in the end that France disgraced themselves when they got to South Africa. They gave the impression that they didn't even want to be there.

There was a real sense of outrage in the studio at the Paris result. The referee was considered completely incompetent but I also thought putting forward the notion that there should be 33 teams at the finals embarrassed Ireland hugely. For the match in Paris, what was never taken into account was, if the tie had finished level and went to penalties, one of our potential penalty takers, Glenn Whelan, had gone off . We mightn't have won anyway but that was completely ignored even if the sense of outrage was justified. Perhaps that papered over the cracks with Trapattoni for a little while.

But aside from his on-pitch performance, for us he is a nightmare to deal with in a television sense because of his lack of English. For one of the matches, Eugene had the idea that we'd have him interviewed in Italian and do our own translation but the idea was abandoned when we were told he was equally confusing in Italian. I was at a function when the mobile operator 3 moved onto soccer and they asked if I'd MC the introduction of Trapattoni to their staff. First I popped along to a press conference though frankly I had no idea what he was talking about most of the time. When it ended I went up to the journalists and said: "I think you guys are fantastic, I don't know how ye interpret that." "Hang on one second, and you'll see the real press conference," they told me. After that they got together and worked out what they thought he was trying to say. It's a nightmare but they soldier on.

So do we all; that's one thing about the Irish soccer team. No matter if it's been good, bad or ugly, they more than any other national team get the nation talking. They've kept us talking year after year and just when you think it can't get any more crazy, something else always happens. The World Cup awaits so we'll see what happens in Rio.

****

As we come to the conclusion, I think about the recognition I've been given through the years. Oddly enough, off the back of Saipan I ended up winning the Sports Journalist of the Year award and it caused controversy because some did not perceive me as a sports journalist at all because I work on television. Paul Howard was one of those in the shake-up with me for the award and he was very gracious about my win. I did not consider my being in the running but I was delighted I won it.

Later on, on vacation in Australia I was contacted by RTÉ who told me they were going to nominate me for TV Personality of the Year, and did I have any objections? Of course I didn't. But I sweated when I learned two of those nominated by other channels were weathermen. What a slagging I'd get from my colleagues if I lost. Happily I won but Après Match get great fun disparaging my award. Let them have their fun, I have the award!

Maybe it was the nerves but I left my wife Hilary in a bad

situation that night. One person at the table knew I had won the award, myself and Hilary had no such knowledge. I wasn't giving the drink a serious lash or anything like that but I was certainly enjoying a few jars. Claire Duignan, who was a senior executive in RTÉ Television at the time and is now in charge of Radio 1, brought Hilary outside, ostensibly to the loo and told her I had won. Claire noticed I was drinking and it concerned her because I would have to go to the stage and make a short speech and wanted to make sure it wasn't a disaster. So Hilary came back and started to subtly drink my drink and keep it away from me. She drank more that night than she intended. When the announcement was made, she burst into tears and that was my drink talking. She always looks back on that as a hugely embarrassing moment in her life.

But working in studio has been far less eventful after a life of covering stories not just across generations, but straddling very different cross-sections of society. The programme inches towards its conclusion and I think of the future. We won't be around forever. But we are fortunate on this panel as we have some great people on the way up who are establishing themselves amongst the institutions that are Dunphy, Brady and Giles.

Ronnie Whelan has huge promise and is progressing all the time. He is serious about his broadcasting and comes in early in the morning when he is on a programme, looks at tapes and picks out incidents he believes to be relevant. He is always well prepared and is becoming stronger and stronger as both an analyst and co-commentator. But one of the difficulties for people coming in — and that would have included people like Ray Houghton, an excellent experienced co-commentator, and Graham Souness — is that in their early days they might have been intimidated by the three lads on the grounds that they are always there and they are so strong and opinionated. It took them a while to learn to be themselves, to stand up for themselves or get walked all over, but they learned well.

What about Roy Keane for the panel — so many put his name forward? I don't think anyone would object but there are some reservations based on his performances across channel. Whether he would work with the lads, I don't know but he's not in a position to call the shots and I'm not sure he brings enough rigour to his analysis. The Irish public has a low tolerance for rubbish so they would expect better lines than banging tables and kicking the door down as an explanation for motivating a performance. There must be a stronger tactical element in his comment, in the opinion of the panel and many involved in football.

Besides, great panels are not always about big names. It's about forthright, honest comment and perhaps my experience with Mick McCarthy proved as much. It wasn't a particularly pleasant one because I said to him: "Mick you must understand one thing about this programme. I don't want any populist viewpoints or someone playing to the gallery and have others on the programme exposed as grumpy old men because they are commenting objectively. So no populism, call it as it is and if you don't, I'll pull you up on it." I say that to everyone joining the programme but Mick didn't like it one bit. He felt I was insulting his integrity but I had a job to do. It was just after he finished as Irish manager and he wouldn't have been a great fan of the programme anyway because of the hard time he got.

Mick has rarely worked with us but a number of new analysts are being developed by Eugene and Ryle Nugent. Richie Sadlier has made a big impact and is one of my favourites. He is not afraid to call it, is tough but fair without being hysterical. He has a great journalistic instinct and in my judgement has a big future as a television analyst. So too Kenny Cunningham, who gets better and better and had a very good Euro 2012. They represent the future with Darragh Maloney, arguably the most comprehensively talented broadcaster in RTÉ Sport, as the anchor who takes over from me.

But hold it there!

We are not going anywhere for some time. While the past has contained a little bit of everything, and the present of tonight's show has gone well, we have our own futures too. Besides, I love live television, those quiet seconds when you can hear your heartbeat outrace the countdown to air and finally you go out in real time to hundreds of thousands of viewers. It will be tough to leave but as of now, that will have to wait for another night as the show comes to an end.

"We'll leave it there so," I say, as the light goes out on the camera and the screen fades to black.

Index

Declan Costello 128
Denis O'Brien 132
Dennis Mitchell 54, 98
Dermot Heneghan 173
Derry 70
Desmond O'Kennedy 123
Dick Hill 40, 99
Dietmar Hamann 140
Dr Dan Connolly 16,17,18
Dr Patrick Hillery's 53
Dundalk 108, 109

E

Eamon 5, 60, 155, 160
Éamon De Valera 62
Eamon Dunphy 3-5, 7, 14, 29,
30-33, 35, 41, 57, 58, 60,
62, 72, 79, 81, 82, 83, 86,
104, 107-109, 117, 135-
137, 139, 140, 143, 144,
146, 149-153, 157, 158,
160, 166, 168, 176, 180,
182
Eamonn Coghlan 178
Emilia Romagna 64
Enda Kenny 129
Enda Marren 93, 127
Eoghan Harris 52
Eoin Neeson 74
Ernest Wood 93
Erskine Childers 65
Eugene O'Neill 3, 4, 117, 135,
136, 141, 160

Euro '88 145
Euro 2012 60, 61
European Championships 31

F

Falls Road 69
Farranferris 16
Fianna Fáil 75
Fine Gael 62, 72, 76, 128, 133
Frank Cluskey 77
Frank Hall 38, 39, 40, 49, 50
Fred Cogley 27, 103, 123, 142,
143, 171
Fr McCarthy 19

G

Garret Cooney 93
Garret FitzGerald 79, 95 127-
129
Gary O'Toole 174, 175, 178,
181
Genoa 157
George Crosbie 45
George Hamilton 7, 29, 60,
143, 156
George Hook 35
George Lee 79, 124, 125
Ger Canning 149
Gerry Fitt 68
Gerry O'Mahony 73
Gerry Ryan 156
Giovanni Trapattoni 60, 61,

149
Glasheen 9, 15
Glen Rovers 11
Golda Meir 63, 65
Graeme Souness 36, 138, 139, 164
Greenmount 10

H

Harry Counihan 119
Harry Thullier 27
Head of Sport 5
Hilary 2, 8, 85, 99, 112, 115, 116, 122, 123, 125, 126, 130
Hilary Patterson 50

I

Ian Paisley 66-68
Ian Ridley 153
IRA 69, 71, 72
Irish Independent 38
Irish Press 15
Irish Times 22, 38, 44, 100
Italia '90 146, 148, 157, 167
ITV 147, 157

J

Jack O'Herlihy 19, 20, 115
Jack Charlton 146, 148-152, 158, 166
Jack Lynch 72, 73, 75, 88, 89
Jack White 45

Jack Young 123, 125
James McClean 158
Jane Mansfield 63
Janet Evans 176
Janet Moody 90
Jayne Mansfield 42
Jenny Westrop 122
Jill 115, 116, 122, 163, 171
Jim Callaghan 183
Jim Carney 145
Jim McGuinness 98, 99, 100, 102, 105
Jim McLaughlin 108
Jimmy Magee 27, 147, 178
Jim Sherwin 177
Joan Fitzgerald 75, 76
Joe Barry 175
Joe Brolly 35
Joe McCarthy 38, 39, 48, 51
Joe McCormack 7, 8, 90, 92, 94, 99
John A Costello 93
John Bruton 132
John Feeney 53
John Giles 3, 4, 14, 29, 30-33, 36, 41, 57, 79, 81, 83, 84, 104, 135, 136, 137, 139, 141, 145, 148, 149, 150, 151, 153, 157, 161, 164, 166, 168, 172, 180
John Healy 128
John Horgan 13, 62, 119, 120, 121
John Hume 68, 70
John O'Donoghue 48

211